PIC MICROCONTROLLER WITH MPLAB AND XC8 PROJECTS HANDSON

High/Low Voltage Detection and Protection, IR Remote, UART Communication, Servo Motor, 7 Segment Display, 16x2 LCD etc..,

Anbazhagan K

CONTENTS

ACKNOWLEDGMENTS

The writer might want to recognize the diligent work of the article group in assembling this book. He might likewise want to recognize the diligent work of the Raspberry Pi Foundation and the Arduino bunch for assembling items and networks that help to make the Internet of Things increasingly open to the overall population. Yahoo for the democratization of innovation!

INTRODUCTION

The Internet of Things (IOT) is a perplexing idea comprised of numerous PCs and numerous correspondence ways. Some IOT gadgets are associated with the Internet and some are most certainly not. Some IOT gadgets structure swarms that convey among themselves. Some are intended for a solitary reason, while some are increasingly universally useful PCs. This book is intended to demonstrate to you the IOT from the back to front. By structure IOT gadgets, the per user will comprehend the essential ideas and will almost certainly develop utilizing the rudiments to make his or her very own IOT applications. These included ventures will tell the per user the best way to assemble their very own IOT ventures and to develop the models appeared. The significance of Computer Security in IOT gadgets is additionally talked about and different systems for protecting the IOT from unapproved clients or programmers. The most significant takeaway from this book is in structure the tasks yourself.

1. HIGH/LOW VOLTAGE DETECTION AND PROTECTION CIRCUIT UTILIZING PIC MICROCONTROLLER

We frequently observe voltage vacillations in power gracefully at our home, which may cause glitch in our home AC apparatuses. Today we are building a minimal effort High and Low Voltage Protection Circuit, which will remove the force gracefully to the apparatuses if there should be an occurrence of High otherwise Low voltage. It will likewise show an alarm message on 16x2 Liquid Crystal Display. In this undertaking, we have utilized PIC Microcontroller to peruse and contrast the info voltage with the reference voltage and make the move in like manner.

We have made this circuit on PCB and included an extra circuit PCB for a similar reason, yet this time utilizing operation amp LM358 (without microcontroller). For exhibit reason, we have picked Low Voltage limit as 150v and high voltage limit as 200v. Here in this undertaking, we haven't utilized any hand-off for cut off, we simply exhibited it utilizing LCD. Be that as it may, the client may join a hand-off with this circuit and associate it with PIC's GPIO.

Further check our other PCB extends here.

Parts Required:

- PIC Microcontroller PIC18F2520

- PCB (requested from EasyEDA)

- IC LM358

- 3 pin Terminal Connector (discretionary)

- 16x2 LCD

- BC547 Transistor

- 1k resistor

- 2k2 resistor

- 30K resistor SMD

- 10k SMD

- Capacitors-0.1uf, 10uF, 1000uF

- 28 pin IC base

- Male/female burgsticks

- 7805 Voltage controllers 7805, 7812

- Pickit2 Programmer

- Driven

- Zener diode-5.1v, 7.5v, 9.2v

- Transformer 12-0-12

- 12MHz Crystal

- 33pF capacitor

- Voltage regulator(fan speed controller)

Functioning Interpretation:

In this High along with Low Voltage Cut Off Circuit, we have perused the AC voltage by utilizing PIC microcontroller with the assistance of transformer, connect rectifier and voltage divider circuit and showed over 16x2 LCD. At that point we have contrasted the AC voltage and as far as possible and showed the alarm message over the LCD in like manner. Like in the event that voltage is underneath 150v, at that point we have indicated "Low Voltage" and on the off chance that voltage is above 200v, at that point we have demonstrated "High Voltage" message over the LCD. We can change those cutoff points in PIC code given toward the finish of this undertaking. Here we have utilized Fan Regulator to increment and reduction the approaching voltage.

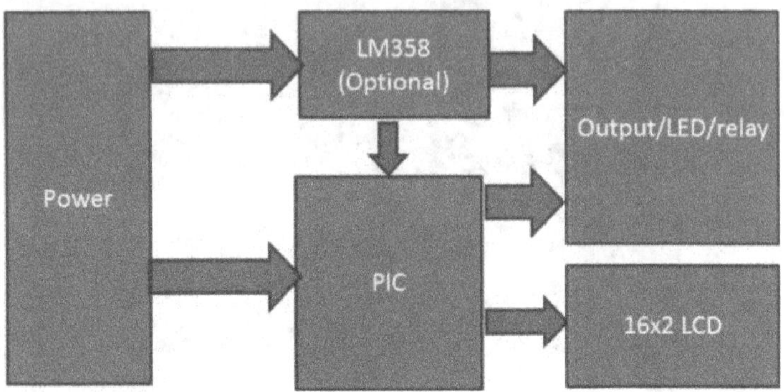

In this circuit, we have additionally included a Simple Under and Over Voltage Protection Circuit without utilizing any microcontroller. In this basic circuit we have utilized LM358 comparator to analyze the info and reference voltage. So here we have three choices in this task:

- Measure and contrast the AC voltage and the assistance of transformer, connect rectifier, voltage divider circuit and PIC microcontroller.

- Identification of over and under voltage by utilizing LM358 with the assistance of transformer, rectifier, and comparator LM358 (without Microcontroller)

- Recognize under and over voltage by utilizing a comparator LM358 and feed its yield to PIC microcontroller for making a move by code.

Here we have shown 1st option of this venture. In which we have ventured down AC input voltage along with afterward changed over that into DC by utilizing an extension rectifier and afterward again mapped this DC voltage to 5v along with afterward ultimately took care of this voltage to PIC microcontroller for examination and show.

In PIC microcontroller we have perused this mapped DC voltage and dependent on that mapped esteem we have determined the approaching AC voltage with the assistance of given equation:

$$volt = ((adcValue*240)/1023)$$

where adcValue is proportionate DC input voltage esteem at PIC controller ADC pin and volt is the applied AC voltage. Here we have accepted 240v as greatest information voltage.

or simultaneously we can utilize given strategy for mapping proportionate DC input esteem.

$$volt = map(adcVlaue, 530, 895, 100, 240)$$

where adcValue is identical DC input voltage esteem at PIC controller ADC pin, 530 is least DC voltage comparable and 895 is most extreme DC voltage equal worth. What's more, 100v is least mapping voltage and 240v is most extreme mapping voltage.

Means 10mV DC contribution at PIC ADC pin is equivalent to 2.046 ADC proportionate worth. So here we have chosen 530 as least worth methods, the voltage at PIC's ADC pin will be:

(((530/2.046)*10)/1000) Volt

2.6v which will be mapped least estimation of 100VAC

(Same estimation for most extreme cutoff).

Check the guide work is given in the PIC program code at long last. Get familiar with Voltage Divider Circuit and mapping the Voltages utilizing ADC here.

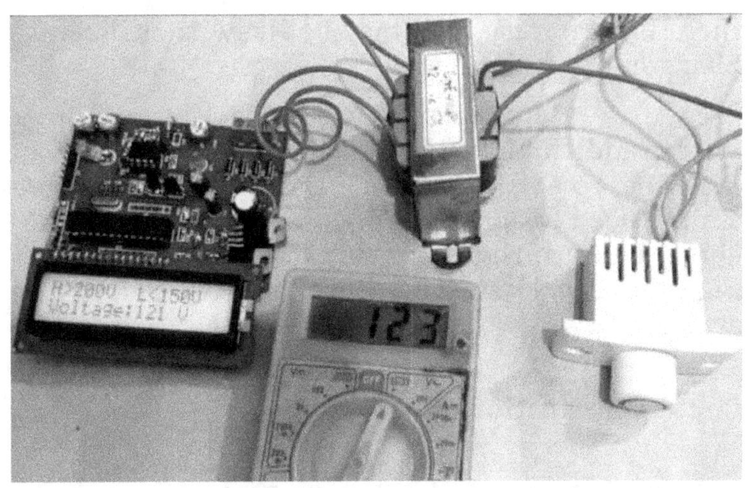

Working of this venture is simple. In this undertaking, we have utilized an AC voltage fan controller for showing it. We have connected fan controller to the contribution of transformer. And afterward by expanding or diminishing its opposition we got wanted voltage yield.

In the code, we have fixed most extreme and least voltage esteems for High voltage and Low voltage discovery. We have fixed 200v as overvoltage limit and 150v as lower voltage limit. Presently subsequent to driving up the circuit, we can view the AC input voltage over the Liquid Crystal Display. At the point when input voltage expands then we can see voltage changes over LCD and in the event that voltage turns out to be more than over voltage limit, at that point LCD will caution us by "HIGH Voltage Alert" and on the off chance that the voltage goes low than under voltage limit, at that point LCD will alarm us by indicating "LOW Voltage Alert" message. Along these lines it very well may be likewise utilized as Electronic Circuit breaker.

We can additionally add a hand-off to append any AC machines to auto cutoff on low or high voltages. We simply need to add a line of code to turn off the machine, beneath the LCD ready message demonstrating code. Check here to utilize Relay with AC apparatuses.

Circuit Explanation:

In High along with low Voltage Protection Circuit, we have utilized a LM358 operation amp which has two yields associated with 2 and 3 number pins of PIC microcontroller. Furthermore, a voltage divider is utilized to isolate voltage and interfaces its yield at fourth number pin of PIC microcontroller. LCD is associated at PORTB of the PIC in 4-piece mode. RS and EN are straightforwardly associated at B0 and B1 and information pins D4, D5, D6 and D7 of LCD are associated at B2, B3, B4 and B5 separately. In this task, we have utilized two voltage controller: 7805 for microcontroller gracefully and 7812 for the LM358 circuit. What's more, a 12v-0-12v advance down transformer is likewise used to step down the AC voltage. Rest of the parts are appeared in the circuit graph underneath.

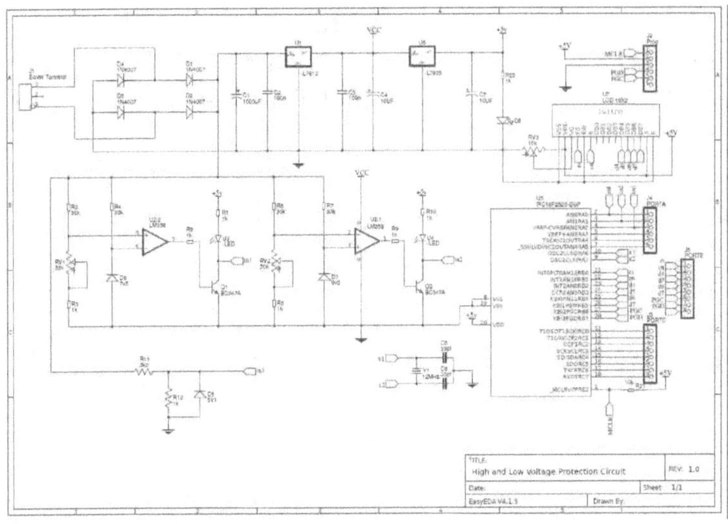

Programming Explanation:

Programming some portion of this undertaking is simple. In this code, we simply need to compute AC voltage by utilizing mapped 0-5v voltage originating from Voltage Divider Circuit and afterward contrast it and predefined values. You can check the total PIC code after this task.

In the 1st place, in the code, we have incorporated a header and designed the PIC microcontroller config bits. On the off chance that you are new to PIC coding, at that point learn PIC Microcontroller and its setup bits here.

At that point we have utilized some fucntions for driving LCD, similar to void lcdbegin() for introducing the LCD, void lcdcmd(char ch) for sending an order to LCD, void lcdwrite(char ch) for sending information to LCD and void lcdprint(char *str) for sending string to LCD. Check all the capacities in the code beneath.

Underneath given capacity is utilized for mapping the qualities:

```
long map(long x, long in_min, long in_max, long out_min, long out_max)

{

  return (x - in_min) * (out_max - out_min) / (in_max - in_min) + out_min;

}
```

Given int analogRead(int ch) work is utilized for introducing and perusing ADC:

```
int analogRead(int ch)

{

    int adcData=0;

    if(ch == 0)
```

```c
    ADCON0 = 0x03;     // adc channel 0

  else if(ch == 1)

    ADCON0 = 0x0b;     //select adc channel 1

  else if(ch == 2)

    ADCON0 = 0x0b;     //select adc channel 2

    ADCON1 = 0b00001100;     // select analog i/p
0,1 and 2 channel of ADC

    ADCON2 = 0b10001010;   //eqisation time hold-
ing cap time

    while(GODONE==1);     // start conversion adc
value

    adcData = (ADRESL)+(ADRESH<<8);   //Store 10-
bit output

    ADON=0;       // adc off

    return adcData;

}
```

Given lines are utilized for getting ADC tests and fig-

ure normal of them and afterward ascertaining voltage:

```
while(1)

{

  long adcValue=0;

  int volt=0;

  for(int i=0;i<100;i++)  // taking samples

   {

    adcValue+=analogRead(2);

    delay(1);

   }

  adcValue/=100;

  #if method == 1

  volt= (((float)adcValue*240.0)/1023.0);

  #else
```

```
volt = map(adcValue, 530, 895, 100, 240);

#endif

sprintf(result,"%d",volt);
```

Lastly given capacity is utilized for making came about move:

```
if(volt > 200)

{

    lcdcmd(1);

    lcdprint("High Voltage");

    lcdcmd(192);

    lcdprint(" Alert ");

    delay(1000);

}

 else if(volt < 150)

{
```

```
    lcdcmd(1);

    lcdprint("Low Voltage");

    lcdcmd(192);

    lcdprint(" Alert ");

    delay(1000);


}
```

Circuit along with Printed Circuit Board Design utilizing EasyEDA:

To plan this HIGH along with LOW Voltage Detector Circuit, we have picked the online EDA instrument called EasyEDA. We have recently utilized EasyEDA ordinarily and thought that it was extremely helpful to utilize contrasted with other PCB fabricators. Check here our all the PCB ventures. EasyEDA isn't just the one stop answer for schematic catch, circuit recreation and PCB plan, they likewise offer an ease PCB Prototype and Components Sourcing administration. They as of late propelled their part sourcing administration where they have a huge load of electronic segments and clients can arrange their necessary segments alongside the PCB request.

While planning your circuits and PCBs, you can similarly make your circuit and PCB structures open so different clients can duplicate or alter them and can take profit by there, we have additionally made our entire Circuit and PCB designs open for this High along with Low Voltage Protection Circuit, check the underneath interface:

The following is the Snapshot of Top layer of Printed Circuit Board design from EasyEDA, you can see any Layer (Top, Bottom, Topsilk, bottomsilk and so on) of the Printed Circuit Board by choosing the layer structure the 'Layers' Window.

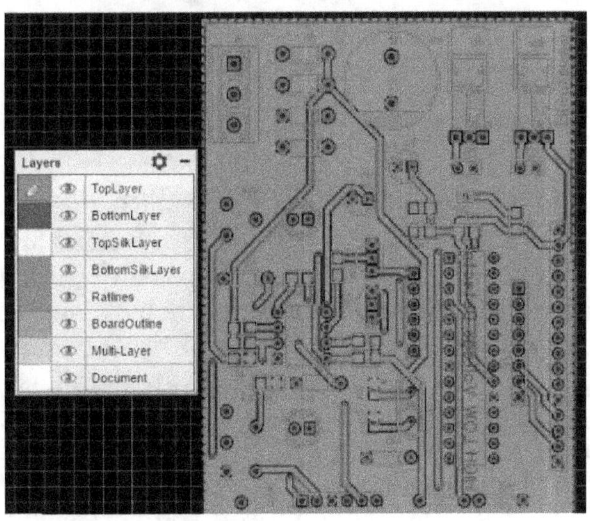

You can likewise checkout the Photo perspective on PCB utilizing EasyEDA:

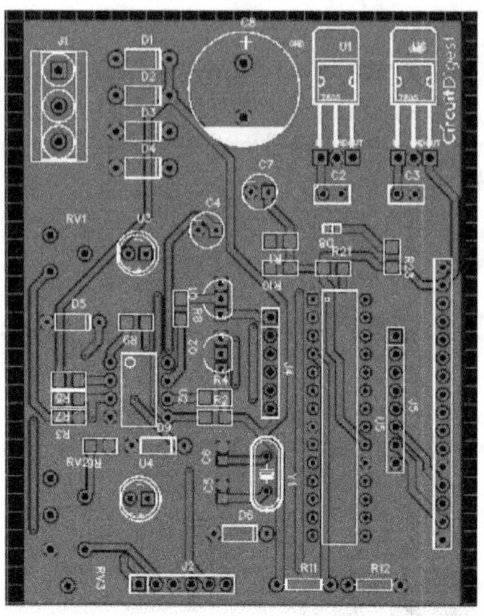

Computing and Ordering PCBs on the web:

In the wake of finishing the plan of PCB, you can tap the symbol of Fabrication yield above. At that point you will get to the page PCB request to download Gerber records of your PCB and send them to any producer, it's additionally significantly simpler (along with cheaper) to arrange it straightforwardly in EasyEDA. Here you can choose the quantity of PCBs you require to arrange, what number of copper layers you need, the PCB thickness, copper weight, and even the PCB shading. After you have chosen the entirety of the choices, click "Spare to Cart" and complete your request, at that point you will get your PCBs a couple of days after the fact. The client may likewise go with their nearby PCB merchant to make PCBs by utilizing Gerber document.

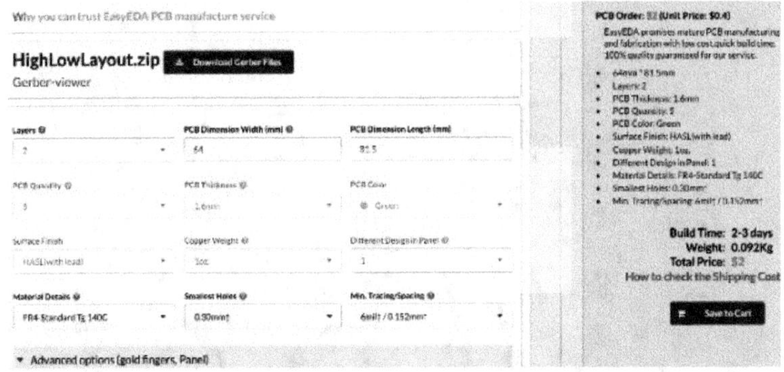

EasyEDA's conveyance is quick and following not many long periods of requesting PCB's I got the PCB tests:

The following are the photos in the wake of patching the segments on PCB:

This how we can without much of a stretch form the Low-high voltage assurance circuit for our home. Further you simply need to add a transfer to associate any AC machines to it, to shield it from voltage variances. Simply interface the hand-off with any broadly useful Pin of PIC MCU and compose the code to make that pin High and low alongside LCD ready message code.

Code

```c
#include<xc.h>     //xc8 is compiler
#include<stdio.h>
#include<stdlib.h>

// CONFIG1H
#pragma config OSC = HS        // Oscillator Selection bits (HS oscillator)
#pragma config FCMEN = OFF     // Fail-Safe Clock
```

Monitor Enable bit (Fail-Safe Clock Monitor disabled)
#pragma config IESO = OFF   // Internal/External Oscillator Switchover bit (Oscillator Switchover mode disabled)

```
// CONFIG2L
#pragma config PWRT = ON     // Power-up Timer Enable bit (PWRT disabled)
#pragma config BOREN = SBORDIS // Brown-out Reset Enable bits (Brown-out Reset enabled in hardware only (SBOREN is disabled))
#pragma config BORV = 3      // Brown Out Reset Voltage bits (Minimum setting)

// CONFIG2H
#pragma config WDT = OFF     // Watchdog Timer Enable bit (WDT disabled (control is placed on the SWDTEN bit))
#pragma config WDTPS = 32768  // Watchdog Timer Postscale Select bits (1:32768)

// CONFIG3H
#pragma config CCP2MX = PORTC   // CCP2 MUX bit (CCP2 input/output is multiplexed with RB1)
#pragma config PBADEN = OFF   // PORTB A/D Enable bit (PORTB<4:0> pins are configured as digital I/O on Reset)
#pragma config LPT1OSC = OFF     // Low-Power Timer1 Oscillator Enable bit (Timer1 configured for higher power operation)
#pragma config MCLRE = ON    // MCLR Pin Enable bit (MCLR pin enabled; RE3 input pin disabled)
```

```
// CONFIG4L
#pragma config STVREN = ON    // Stack Full/Under-
flow Reset Enable bit (Stack full/underflow will cause
Reset)
#pragma config LVP = OFF      // Single-Supply ICSP
Enable bit (Single-Supply ICSP disabled)
#pragma config XINST = OFF    // Extended Instruc-
tion Set Enable bit (Instruction set extension and In-
dexed Addressing mode disabled (Legacy mode))

// CONFIG5L
#pragma config CP0 = OFF      // Code Protection bit
(Block 0 (000800-001FFFh) not code-protected)
#pragma config CP1 = OFF      // Code Protection bit
(Block 1 (002000-003FFFh) not code-protected)
#pragma config CP2 = OFF      // Code Protection bit
(Block 2 (004000-005FFFh) not code-protected)
#pragma config CP3 = OFF      // Code Protection bit
(Block 3 (006000-007FFFh) not code-protected)

// CONFIG5H
#pragma config CPB = OFF      // Boot Block Code Pro-
tection bit (Boot block (000000-0007FFh) not code-
protected)
#pragma config CPD = OFF      // Data EEPROM Code
Protection bit (Data EEPROM not code-protected)

// CONFIG6L
#pragma config WRT0 = OFF    // Write Protection bit
(Block 0 (000800-001FFFh) not write-protected)
#pragma config WRT1 = OFF    // Write Protection bit
(Block 1 (002000-003FFFh) not write-protected)
```

```
#pragma config WRT2 = OFF    // Write Protection bit
(Block 2 (004000-005FFFh) not write-protected)
#pragma config WRT3 = OFF    // Write Protection bit
(Block 3 (006000-007FFFh) not write-protected)

// CONFIG6H
#pragma config WRTC = OFF        // Configuration
Register Write Protection bit (Configuration registers
(300000-3000FFh) not write-protected)
#pragma config WRTB = OFF     // Boot Block Write
Protection bit (Boot block (000000-0007FFh) not
write-protected)
#pragma config WRTD = OFF    // Data EEPROM Write
Protection bit (Data EEPROM not write-protected)

// CONFIG7L
#pragma config EBTR0 = OFF     // Table Read Pro-
tection bit (Block 0 (000800-001FFFh) not protected
from table reads executed in other blocks)
#pragma config EBTR1 = OFF     // Table Read Pro-
tection bit (Block 1 (002000-003FFFh) not protected
from table reads executed in other blocks)
#pragma config EBTR2 = OFF     // Table Read Pro-
tection bit (Block 2 (004000-005FFFh) not protected
from table reads executed in other blocks)
#pragma config EBTR3 = OFF     // Table Read Pro-
tection bit (Block 3 (006000-007FFFh) not protected
from table reads executed in other blocks)

// CONFIG7H
#pragma config EBTRB = OFF    // Boot Block Table
Read Protection bit (Boot block (000000-0007FFh)
```

not protected from table reads executed in other blocks)

```
#define rs RB0
#define en RB1
char result[10];
#define lcdport PORTB
#define method 0

void delay(unsigned int Delay)
{
  int i,j;
  for(i=0;i<Delay;i++)
    for(j=0;j<1000;j++);
}

void lcdcmd(char ch)
{
  lcdport= (ch>>2)& 0x3C;
  rs=0;
  en=1;
  delay(1);
  en=0;
  lcdport= (ch<<2) & 0x3c;
  rs=0;
  en=1;
  delay(1);
  en=0;
}

void lcdwrite(char ch)
{
  lcdport=(ch>>2) & 0x3c;
```

```c
 rs=1;
 en=1;
 delay(1);
 en=0;
 lcdport=(ch<<2) & 0x3c;
 rs=1;
 en=1;
 delay(1);
 en=0;
}

void lcdprint(char *str)
{
  while(*str)
  {
    lcdwrite(*str);
    str++;
  }
}

void lcdbegin()
{
  lcdcmd(0x02);
  lcdcmd(0x28);
  lcdcmd(0x0e);
  lcdcmd(0x06);
  lcdcmd(0x01);
}

int analogRead(int ch)
{
  int adcData=0;
```

```c
  if(ch == 0)
  ADCON0 = 0x03;    // adc channel 0
  else if(ch == 1)
  ADCON0 = 0x0b;    //select adc channel 1
  else if(ch == 2)
  ADCON0 = 0x0b;    //select adc channel 2
   ADCON1 = 0b00001100;   // select analog i/p   0,1
and 2 channel of ADC
   ADCON2 = 0b10001010;   //eqisation time holding
cap time
  while(GODONE==1);   // start conversion adc value
  adcData = (ADRESL)+(ADRESH<<8);   //Store 10-bit
output
  ADON=0;       // adc off
  return adcData;
}

long  map(long  x, long  in_min, long  in_max, long
out_min, long out_max)
{
 return (x - in_min) * (out_max - out_min) / (in_max -
in_min) + out_min;
}

void main()
{
//ADCON1  = 0b0001111;   //all port is digital
TRISB=0x00;
TRISC=0x00;
TRISA=0xff;
lcdbegin();
lcdprint("HIGH/LOW Volt");
```

```c
lcdcmd(192);
lcdprint("Detector by PIC");
delay(1000);
lcdcmd(1);
lcdprint("Hello world");
lcdcmd(192);
lcdprint("Welcomes You");
delay(1000);

while(1)
{
  long adcValue=0;
  int volt=0;
  for(int i=0;i<100;i++)  // taking samples
  {
    adcValue+=analogRead(2);
    delay(1);
  }
  adcValue/=100;

  #if method == 1
  volt= (((float)adcValue*240.0)/1023.0);
  #else
  volt = map(adcValue, 530, 895, 100, 240);
  #endif
  sprintf(result,"%d",volt);


    lcdcmd(0x80);
  lcdprint("H>200V L<150V");
  lcdcmd(0xc0);
  lcdprint("Voltage:");
```

```
    lcdprint(result);
    lcdprint(" V ");
    delay(1000);
    if(volt > 200)
    {
      lcdcmd(1);
      lcdprint("High Voltage");
      lcdcmd(192);
      lcdprint(" Alert ");
      delay(1000);
    }


      else if(volt < 150)
    {
      lcdcmd(1);
      lcdprint("Low Voltage");
      lcdcmd(192);
      lcdprint(" Alert ");
      delay(1000);
    }
}
}
```

◆ ◆ ◆

2. IR REMOTE CONTROLLED HOME AUTOMATION UTILIZING PIC MICROCON-TROLLER

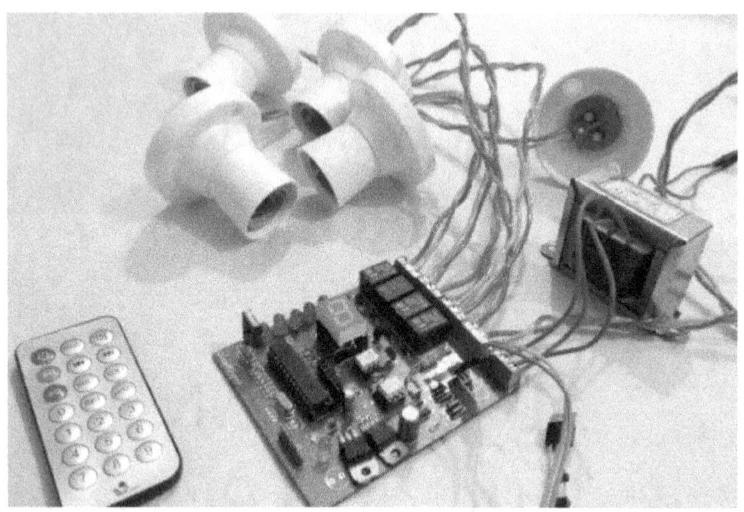

In this task, we are gonna to utilize a PIC micro-controller to remotely control not many AC stacks by simply utilizing an IR remote. A comparable undertaking IR remote controlled Home mechanization has just been finished with Arduino additionally, however here we structured it on PCB utilizing EasyEDA's online PCB planner and test system, and utilized their PCB structuring administrations to arrange the PCB sheets as appeared in the ensuing area of the article.

Toward the finish of this venture you will have the option to flip (ON/OFF) any AC load utilizing a conventional Remote from the solace of your Chair/Bed. To cause this undertaking all the more fascinating we to have additionally empowered a component to control the speed of the fan with the assistance of Triac. All these should be possible with straightforward taps on your IR remote. You can use any of your TV/DVD/MP3 remote for this task. The distinctive IR signals from the remote are gotten by the microcontroller which at that point controls the particular transfers by means of a hand-off driver circuit. These transfers are utilized to associate and separate the AC Loads (Lights/Fan).

Working Explanation:

The working of this venture is genuinely easy to comprehend. At the point when a catch is pushed on the IR Remote it sends a succession of code in type of encoded beats utilizing 38Khz adjusting recurrence. These heartbeats are gotten by the TSOP1738 sensor along with afterward read by the Controller. The Controller at that point translates the got train of the beats into a hex worth and contrasts it and the predefined hex qualities in our program.

On the off chance that any match happens, at that point the controller plays out a relative activity by setting off the particular Relay/Triac and the comparing result is additionally demonstrated by ready LEDs. Here in this undertaking, we have utilized 4 bulbs (little bulbs) of various hues as lighting loads and another bulb (greater bulb) is viewed as a fan for exhibition reason.

We have chosen key 1 to flip the relay1, 2 to flip the relay2, 3 to flip the relay3, 4 to flip the relay4, and Vol + to speed up and Vol- to diminish speed of the fan.

Note: Here we have utilized 100watt bulb rather than a fan.

There are numerous sorts of IR Remotes accessible for various gadgets, yet a large portion of them work around 38KHz Frequency. Here in this task, we control home apparatuses utilizing IR TV remote and for recognizing the IR signals, we utilize a TSOP1738 IR Receiver. This TSOP1738 sensor can detect 38Khz Frequency signal. The working of IR remote along with the TSOP1738 is canvassed in detail in this article: IR Transmitter along with Receiver

Our PIC microcontroller works at +5V along with the Relays work at +12V, Hence we utilize a transformer to step down the 220V AC along with redress it utilizing a full scaffold rectifier. This amended DC voltage is then managed to +12V and +5V by utilizing the controller ICs 7812 and 7805 separately.

To trigger the hand-off we utilize transistors like BC547 which can go about as an electronic change to turn ON/OFF the transfers dependent on the sign from the PIC microcontroller.Further to manage the speed of the fan we are utilizing a TRIAC. TRIAC is a force semiconductor which is fit for managing the yield voltage; this capacity is utilized to control the speed of the fan.

We have additionally utilized a Triac Driver to control the Triac utilizing our PIC microcontroller. This driver is utilized to give a terminating edge heartbeat to Triac, with the goal that the yield force can be managed. Here we have utilized 6 degree of speed control. At the point when the level is 0 then the fan will be off. At the point when level will be 1 at that point speed will be 1/fifth of max throttle. At the point when level will be 2 at that point speed will be 2/fifth of max throttle and individually for other people. The present degree of the speed can be observed utilizing the on-board 7-fragment show.

The square chart of the task is demonstrated as follows.

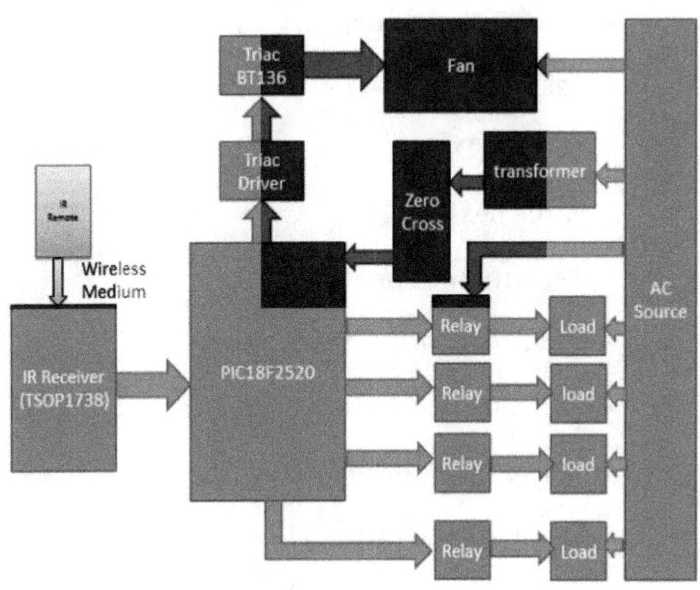

Parts:

The parts required to fabricate this venture is given underneath:

- PIC18f2520 Microcontroller - 1
- TSOP1738 - 1
- IR TV/DVD Remote - 1
- Transistor BC547 - 4
- Transfers 12 volt - 4
- Bulb with holder - 5
- Associating wires -
- EasyEda PCB - 1
- 16x2 LCD
- Force flexibly 12v
- Terminal connector 2 pin'- 8
- Terminal Connector 3 pin - 1
- Transformer 12-0-12 - 1 -
- Voltage Regulator 7805 - 1
- Voltage Regulator 7812 - 1

- Capacitor 1000uf - 1
- Capacitor 10uf - 1
- Capacitor 0.1uf - 1
- Capacitor 0.01uf 400V ' - 1
- 10k - 5
- 1k - 5
- 100ohm - 7
- Basic cathode fragment - 1
- 1n4007 diode - 10
- BT136 triac - 1
- Male/female header -
- LEDs - 6
- Opto-coupler moc3021 - 1
- Opto-coupler mtc2e otherwise 4n35 - 1
- 20Mhz precious stone - 1
- 33pf capacitor - 2
- 5.1v zener diode - 1
- 47 ohm 2 watt resistor - 1

Every one of these segments are usually utilized and

can be effortlessly bought. Be that as it may in case you are searching for a best purchase on the web, at that point we would suggest you LCSC.

LCSC is an extraordinary online store to purchase your gadgets parts for a large range of tasks. They include around 25,000 sorts of segments and interestingly, they sell even little amount things for little tasks and they additionally have Global Shipping.

Interpreting the IR Remote:

As said before you can utilize any benevolent remote for your venture. However, we need to recognize what sort of sign is produced for from that specific remote. For each individual key on the remote there will be an identical HEX an incentive for that key. Utilizing this HEX worth we can recognize each key on our microcontroller side. So before we choose to utilize a remote we should know the HEX an incentive for the keys preset in that specific remote. In this undertaking, we have utilized a NEC remote. The HEX qualities for the keys on a NEC remote is given underneath.

Decimal	Hex	key
33441975	1FE48B7	OFF
33446055	1FE58A7	mode
33454215	1FE7887	mute
33456255	1FE807F	resume
33439935	1FE40BF	previous
33472575	1FEC03F	next
33431775	1FE20DF	EQ
33464415	1FEA05F	volume -
33448095	1FE609F	volume +
33480735	1FEE01F	0
33427695	1FE10EF	RPT
33460335	1FE906F	U/SD
33444015	1FE50AF	1
33478695	1FED827	2
33486855	1FEF807	3
33435855	1FE30CF	4
33468495	1FEB04F	5
33423615	1FE00FF	6
33452175	1FE708F	7
33484815	1FEF00F	8
33462375	1FE9867	9

As you can view the HEX worth has 7 characters out of which just the last two varies, consequently we can consider just the last two digits to recognize every keys.

	key
B7	OFF
A7	mode
87	mute
7F	resume
BF	previous
3F	next
DF	EQ
5F	volume -
9F	volume +
1F	0
EF	RPT
6F	U/SD
AF	1
27	2
07	3
CF	4
4F	5
FF	6
8F	7
0F	8
67	9

Circuit Diagram:

The schematic for the undertaking is demonstrated as follows.

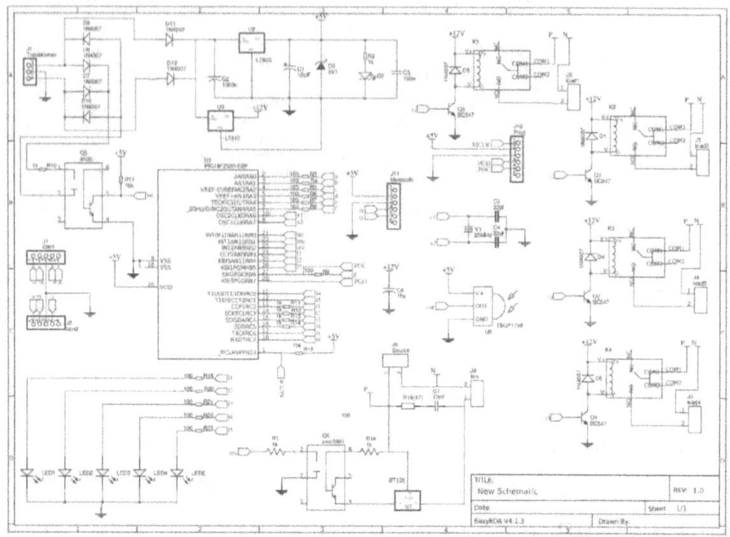

The above schematic was made simple by utilizing esayEDA schematic editorial manager since they give the designs of all parts utilized in this venture. It additionally doesn't require an establishment and can be used online in a hurry.

The pinouts and part esteems are obviously determined in the schematic above. You can similarly download the schematic document from here.

Programming:

The program for this undertaking is completed using MPLABX, the code is additionally really basic and straightforward. The total code will be given toward the finish of this instructional exercise, further barely any significant pieces of the program are clarified beneath.

In the start of the code, we must incorporate required libraries, characterize the pins and proclaim the factors.

```
#include <xc.h>

#include<string.h>

#include<stdlib.h>

#include "config.h"

#define tric RB1

#define ir RB2

#define relay1 RC2

#define relay2 RC3

#define relay3 RC4

#define relay4 RC5

#define rly1LED RB3

#define rly2LED RB4
```

```
#define rly3LED RB5

#define rly4LED RC1

#define fanLED RC0

int flag=0;

int cmd=0;

int speed=5;

unsigned int dat[100];

int i=0;

char result[10];

int j=0;
```

From that point forward, we have made a basic defer work by utilizing the "for" circle.

```
void delay(int time)

{

    for(int i=0;i<time;i++)
```

```
    for(int j=0;j<800;j++);

}
```

From that point forward, we have introduced the clock by utilizing the accompanying capacity

```
void timer()       // 10 -> 1us

{

  TOPSO=0;

  TOPS1=0;

  TOPS2=0;

  PSA=0;    //Timer Clock Source is from Prescaler

  TOCS=0;        //Prescaler gets clock from FCPU (5MHz)

  TO8BIT=0;  //16 BIT MODE

  TMROIE=1;  //Enable TIMERO Interrupt

  PEIE=1;   //Enable Peripheral Interrupt

  GIE=1;    //Enable INTs globally
```

```
    TMR0ON=1;    //Now start the timer!


}
```

Presently in the fundamental capacity, we have offer bearings to the chose sticks and introduce clock and outside intrude on int0 to distinguish zero intersection.

```
ADCON1=0b00001111;

  TRISB1=0;

  TRISB2=1;

  TRISB3=0;

  TRISB4=0;

  TRISB5=0;

  TRISC=0x00;

  TRISA=0x00;

  PORTA=0xc0;

  TRISB6=0;
```

```c
RB6=1;

relay1=0;

relay2=0;

relay3=0;

relay4=0;

rly1LED=0;

rly3LED=0;

rly2LED=0;

rly4LED=0;

fanLED=0;

   i=0;

ir=0;

tric=0;

timer();

INTEDG0 = 0; // Interrupt on falling edge
```

```
    INTOIE = 1; // Enable the INT0 external interrupt
(RB0)

    INTOIF = 0; // Clears INT0 External Interrupt Flag
bit

    PEIE=1;   //Enable Peripheral Interrupt

    GIE=1;    //Enable INTs globally
```

Presently, here we are not utilizing any hinder or catch and contrast mode with recognize IR signal. Here we have quite recently utilized a computerized pin to peruse information simply like we read a press button. At whatever point signal goes high or low we simply put debouncing technique and run the clock. At whatever point pin changes its state to another at that point time esteems will be spared in an exhibit.

IR remote send rationale 0 as 562.5us and rationale 1 as 2250us. At whatever point clock peruses around 562.5us then we expect it 0 and when clock peruses around 2250us then we accept it as 1. At that point we convert it in hex.

The approaching sign from remote contains 34 bits. We store all the bytes in the exhibit and afterward translate the last byte to utilize.

```
  while(ir == 1);
```

```c
INTOIE = 0;

while(ir == 0);

TMR0=0;

while(ir == 1);

i++;

dat[i]=TMR0;

if(dat[1] > 5000 && dat[1]<12000)

{

}
else
{

    i=0;

    INTOIE = 1;

}

if(i>=33)
```

```c
    {

    GIE=0;

    delay(50);

    cmd=0;

    for(j=26;j<34;j++)

    {

        if(dat[j]>1000 && dat[j]<2000)

            cmd<<=1;

        else if(dat[j]>3500 && dat[j]<4500)

        {

            cmd|=0x01;

            cmd<<=1;

        }

    }

    cmd>>=1;
```

The above bit of code gets and interprets the IR signal utilizing clock hinders and stores the relating HEX an incentive in the variable cmd. Presently we can think about this HEX worth (cmd variable) with our predefined HEX qualities and flip the transfer as indicated below

```
if(cmd == 0xAF)

    {

        relay1=~relay1;

        rly1LED=~rly1LED;

    }

    else if(cmd == 0x27)

    {

        relay2=~relay2;

        rly2LED=~rly2LED;

    }

    else if(cmd == 0x07)
```

```c
        {

            relay3=~relay3;

            rly3LED=~rly3LED;

        }

    else if(cmd == 0xCF)

        {

            relay4=~relay4;

            rly4LED=~rly4LED;

        }

    else if(cmd == 0x5f)

        {

        speed++;

        if(speed>5)

            {

                speed=5;
```

```
        }


    }

    else if(cmd == 0x9f)

    {

        speed--;

        if(speed<=0)

        {

            speed=0;

        }

    }
```

Now to know at which our fan is right now working, we should utilize a 7-fragment show. The accompanying lines are utilized to educate the pins of the 7-fragment show.

```
if(speed == 5)    // turned off 5x2= 10ms triger  // speed 0

    {
```

```c
        PORTA=0xC0;       // display 0

    RB6=1;

    fanLED=0;

}

else if(speed == 4 )  // 8 ms trigger  //speed 1

{

   PORTA=0xfc;    // displaying 1

   RB6=1;

   fanLED=1;

}

else if(speed == 3) //  6 ms trigger   // speed 2

{

   PORTA=0xE4;   // displaying 2

   RB6=0;

   fanLED=1;
```

```c
    }

    else if(speed == 2)  // 4ms trigger // speed 3

    {

        PORTA=0xF0;    // displaying 3

        RB6=0;

        fanLED=1;

    }

    else if(speed == 1)  // 2ms trigger // speed 4

    {

        PORTA=0xD9;     // displaying 4

        RB6=0;

        fanLED=1;

    }

    else if(speed == 0)     // 0ms trigger // speed 5
full power

    {
```

```
    PORTA=0xD2;      // displaying 5

    RB6=0;

    fanLED=1;

}
```

The beneath work is for outside hinder and time flood. This capacity is answerable for identifying zero intersection and driving the Triac.

```
void interrupt isr()

{

  if(INT0IF)

  {

    delay(speed);

    tric=1;

    for(int t=0;t<100;t++);

    tric=0;

    INT0IF=0;
```

```
    }

    if(TMR0IF)  //Check if it is TMR0 Overflow ISR

    {

       TMR0IF=0;

    }

}
```

The last PCB for this IR remote controlled home computerization looks as demonstrated as follows:

Circuit and PCB Design utilizing EasyEDA:

To structure this Remote control home computerization we have utilized EasyEDA which is a free online EDA instrument for making circuits and PCBs in a consistent way. We have recently requested not many PCBs from EasyEDA and as yet utilizing their administrations as we found the entire procedure, from attracting the circuits to requesting the PCBs, increasingly advantageous and productive in correlation of other PCB fabricators. EasyEDA offers circuit drawing, reproduction, PCB configuration for nothing and furthermore offers high caliber however low value Customized PCB administration. Check here for the total instructional exercise on How to utilize Easy EDA for making Schematics, PCB designs, Simulating the Circuits and so on.

EasyEDA is improving step by step; they have included numerous new highlights and improved the general client experience, which makes EasyEDA simpler and usable for structuring circuits. They are before long going to dispatch its Desktop variant, which can be downloaded and introduced on your PC for disconnected use.

In EasyEDA, you can make your circuit and PCB plans open with the goal that different clients can duplicate or alter them and can take profit by there, we have likewise made our entire Circuit and PCB formats open for this Remote control Home robotization.

The following is the Snapshot of Top layer of Printed Circuit Board design from EasyEDA, you can view any Layer (Top, Bottom, Topsilk, bottomsilk and so forth) of the PCB by choosing the layer structure the 'Layers' Window.

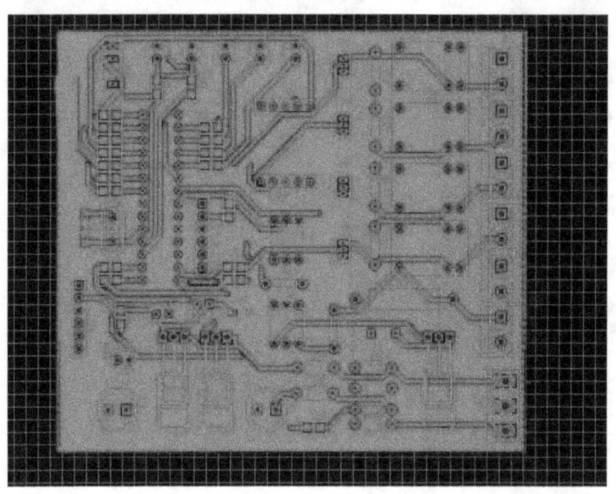

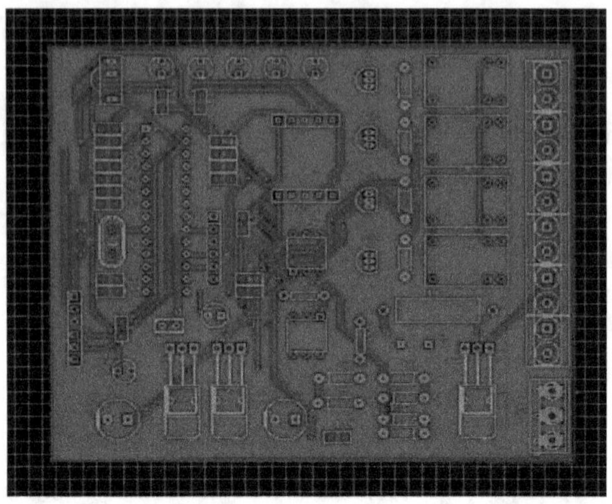

Figuring and Ordering PCB Samples on the web:

In the wake of finishing the structure of PCB, you can tap the symbol of Fabrication yield, which will take you on the PCB request page. Here you can see your PCB in Gerber Viewer otherwise download Gerber documents of your PCB and send them to any maker, it's additionally much simpler (and less expensive) to arrange it legitimately in EasyEDA. Here you can choose the quantity of PCBs you require to arrange, what number of copper layers you need, the PCB thickness, copper weight, and even the PCB shading. After you have chosen the entirety of the alternatives, click "Spare to Cart" and complete your request, at that point you will get your PCBs inside hardly any days.

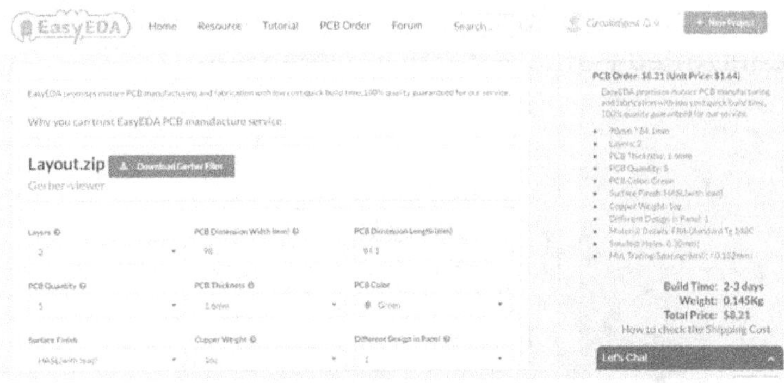

You can legitimately arrange this PCB or download the Gerber record utilizing this connection.

Following barely any long periods of requesting PCB's we got the PCBs. The sheets that we got are demonstrated as follows.

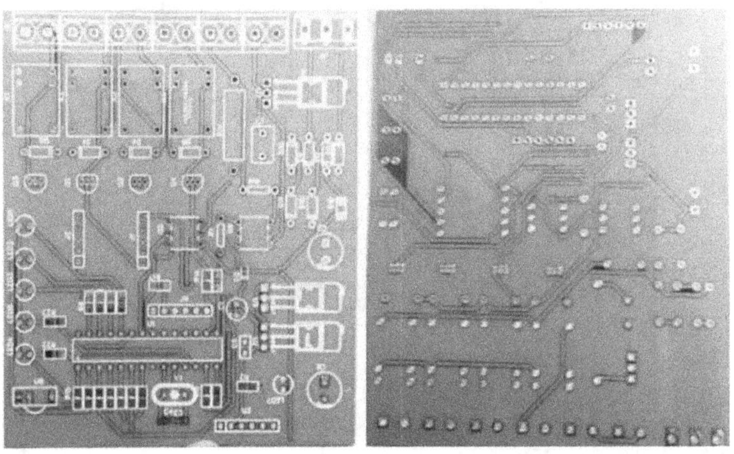

When we got the PCBs I mounted all the necessary

segments over the PCB, lastly we have our IR Remote Controlled Home Automation prepared.

Code

```c
#include <xc.h>
#include<string.h>
#include<stdlib.h>
```

```c
#include "config.h"

#define tric RB1
#define ir RB2

#define relay1 RC2
#define relay2 RC3
#define relay3 RC4
#define relay4 RC5

#define rly1LED RB3
#define rly2LED RB4
#define rly3LED RB5
#define rly4LED RC1
#define fanLED RC0

int flag=0;
int cmd=0;
int speed=5;
unsigned int dat[100];
int i=0;
char result[10];
int j=0;


void delay(int time)
{
  for(int i=0;i<time;i++)
    for(int j=0;j<800;j++);
}

void timer()      // 10 -> 1us
{
  T0PS0=0;
```

```c
 T0PS1=0;
 T0PS2=0;
 PSA=0;    //Timer Clock Source is from Prescaler
 T0CS=0;   //Prescaler gets clock from FCPU (5MHz)
 T08BIT=0;  //16 BIT MODE
 TMR0IE=1; //Enable TIMER0 Interrupt
 PEIE=1;   //Enable Peripheral Interrupt
 GIE=1;    //Enable INTs globally
 TMR0ON=1;    //Now start the timer!
}

void main(void)
{
 ADCON1=0b00001111;
 TRISB1=0;
 TRISB2=1;
 TRISB3=0;
 TRISB4=0;
 TRISB5=0;
 TRISC=0x00;
 TRISA=0x00;
 PORTA=0xc0;
 TRISB6=0;
 RB6=1;
 relay1=0;
 relay2=0;
 relay3=0;
 relay4=0;
 rly1LED=0;
 rly3LED=0;
 rly2LED=0;
```

```c
rly4LED=0;
fanLED=0;
  i=0;
ir=0;
tric=0;
timer();
INTEDG0 = 0; // Interrupt on falling edge
 INTOIE = 1; // Enable the INT0 external interrupt
(RB0)
INTOIF = 0; // Clears INT0 External Interrupt Flag bit
PEIE=1;   //Enable Peripheral Interrupt
GIE=1;    //Enable INTs globally

while(1)
{
  while(ir == 1);
  INTOIE = 0;
  while(ir == 0);
  TMR0=0;
  while(ir == 1);
  i++;
  dat[i]=TMR0;


    if(dat[1] > 5000 && dat[1]<12000)
  {
  }
  else
  {
    i=0;
    INTOIE = 1;
```

```c
}
if(i>=33)
{
GIE=0;
delay(50);
cmd=0;
for(j=26;j<34;j++)
{
  if(dat[j]>1000 && dat[j]<2000)
    cmd<<=1;

  else if(dat[j]>3500 && dat[j]<4500)
  {
    cmd|=0x01;
    cmd<<=1;
  }
}
cmd>>=1;


    if(cmd == 0xAF)
  {
   relay1=~relay1;
   rly1LED=~rly1LED;
  }


    else if(cmd == 0x27)
  {
   relay2=~relay2;
   rly2LED=~rly2LED;
```

```c
}


    else if(cmd == 0x07)
{
  relay3=~relay3;
  rly3LED=~rly3LED;
}


    else if(cmd == 0xCF)
{
  relay4=~relay4;
  rly4LED=~rly4LED;
}


    else if(cmd == 0x5f)
{
  speed++;
  if(speed>5)
  {
    speed=5;
  }
}


    else if(cmd == 0x9f)
{
  speed--;
  if(speed<=0)
  {
```

```c
        speed=0;
     }
  }


    if(speed == 5)     // turned off  5x2 = 10ms triger
//speed 0
   {
   PORTA=0xC0;      // display 0
   RB6=1;
     fanLED=0;
   }


    else if(speed == 4 )  // 8 ms trigger  //speed 1
  {
  PORTA=0xfc;    // displaying 1
  RB6=1;
     fanLED=1;
  }


    else if(speed == 3)  //  6 ms trigger   // speed 2
  {
  PORTA=0xE4;    // displaying 2
  RB6=0;
     fanLED=1;
  }


    else if(speed == 2)  // 4ms trigger // speed 3
  {
```

```c
    PORTA=0xF0;    // displaying 3
    RB6=0;
    fanLED=1;
}


    else if(speed == 1)  // 2ms trigger // speed 4
{
  PORTA=0xD9;     // displaying 4
  RB6=0;
  fanLED=1;
}


    else if(speed == 0)     // 0ms trigger // speed 5
full power
  {
  PORTA=0xD2;      // displaying 5
  RB6=0;
  fanLED=1;
  }


    else
{
  RB6=1;
  PORTA=0xff;    // display off
  fanLED=0;
}

    i=0;
```

```c
      INTOIE = 1;
      GIE=1;
      }
}
}

void interrupt isr()
{
  if(INTOIF)
  {
    delay(speed);
    tric=1;
    for(int t=0;t<100;t++);
    tric=0;
    INTOIF=0;
  }


  if(TMROIF) //Check if it is TMR0 Overflow ISR
  {
  TMROIF=0;
  }


}
```

◆ ◆ ◆

3. INTERFACING BLUETOOTH MODULE HC-06 WITH PIC MICROCONTROLLER

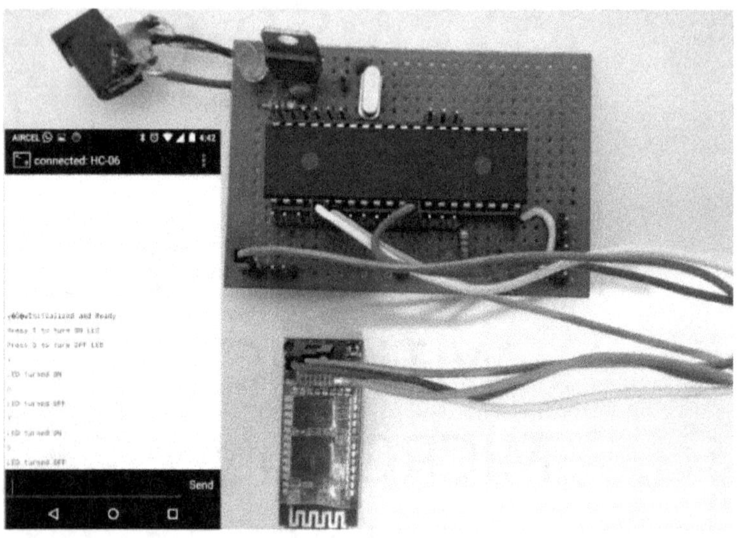

In this instructional exercise we will figure out How to make out PIC ventures remote by interfacing a Bluetooth Module (HC-06). In our past instructional exercise we have as of now figured out How to utilize USART module in our PIC Microcontroller and built up correspondence among PIC and Computer. In case you are a flat out learner, at that point check here for our all the PIC Tutorials, where we have begun from the scratch, such as learning MPLAB and XC8, interfacing LED, LCD, utilizing Timers, ADC, PWM and so forth.

Here, we have utilized the well known Bluetooth module HC-06. Utilizing this module we can get and send data remotely from our PIC MCU to a versatile application or a PC. Correspondence among PIC and HC-06 is set up utilizing the USART module present in the PIC Microcontroller. You can likewise utilize the HC-05. We again work on the equivalent Asynchronous 8-piece mode, however this time we will alter our code a piece so it works with the Bluetooth module. Consequently learning UART instructional exercise heretofore is an additional preferred position for this task.

In this instructional exercise, we will flip a LED by sending on or off order from our Smart telephone. We will utilize an Android application called Bluetooth Terminal which can send and get information over Bluetooth. On the off chance that we send a burn '1' from the application the light will be turned ON in the PIC board and we will recover an affirmation to the telephone that the light has been turned on. Correspondingly we can send '0' from telephone to turn it off. In this way we can control the LED light on our PIC board, like the UART instructional exercise yet now remotely. Complete Program is given toward the finish of this instructional exercise.

The essential square outline for the arrangement is demonstrated as follows.

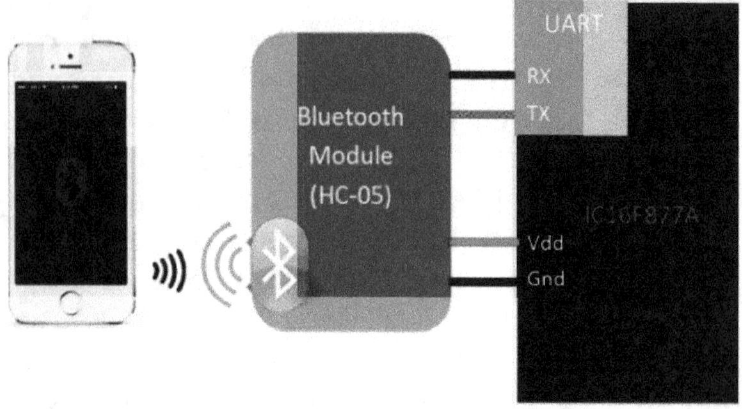

Necessities:

Equipment:

- PIC16F877A Perf Board

- HC-05 or HC-06 Bluetooth Module

- PC (for programming)

- Cell Phone

- PICkit 3 Programmer

Programming:

- MPLABX

- Bluetooth Terminal (Mobile Application)

Bluetooth Module HC-06:

Bluetooth can work in the accompanying two modes:

- Order Mode

- Working Mode

In Command Mode we will have the option to arrange the Bluetooth properties like the name of the Bluetooth signal, its secret word, the working baud rate and so forth. The Operating Mode is the one wherein we will have the option to send and get information between the PIC Microcontroller and the Bluetooth module. Thus in this instructional exercise we will toy just with the Operating Mode. The Command mode will be left to the default settings. The Device name will be HC-05 (I am utilizing HC-06) and the secret word will be 0000 or 1234 and in particular the default baud rate for all Bluetooth modules will be 9600.

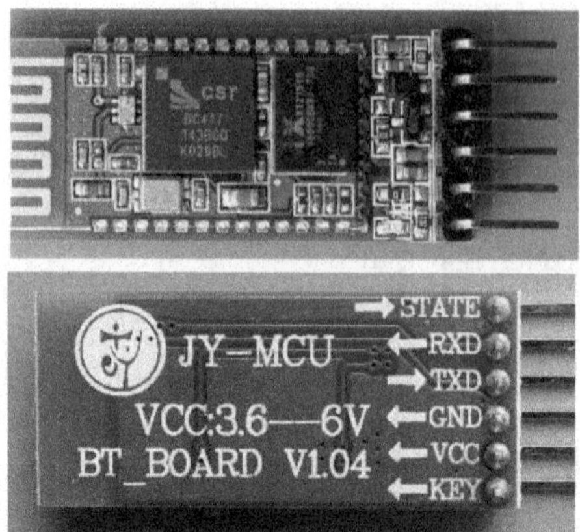

The module chips away at 5V gracefully and the sign pins work on 3.3V, thus a 3.3V controller is available in the module itself. Consequently we need not stress over it. Out of the six pins just four will be utilized in the Operating mode. The pin association table is demonstrated as follows

S.No	Pin on HC-05/ HC-06	Pin name on MCU	Pin number in PIC
1	Vcc	Vdd	31st pin
2	Vcc	Gnd	32nd pin
3	Tx	RC6/Tx/CK	25th pin
4	Rx	RC7/Rx/DT	26th pin

| 5 | State | NC | NC |
| 6 | EN (Enable) | NC | NC |

Check our different undertakings to get familiar with Bluetooth module HC-05 with different microcontrollers:

- Bluetooth Controlled Toy Car utilizing Arduino

- Bluetooth Controlled Home Automation System utilizing 8051

- Voice Controlled Lights utilizing Raspberry Pi

- Advanced cell Controlled FM Radio utilizing Arduino and Processing

- Cell Phone Controlled Robot Car utilizing G-Sensor along with Arduino

Programming PIC Microcontroller for Bluetooth Communication:

Like all modules (ADC, Timer, PWM) we must likewise introduce our Bluetooth module. The introduction will be like UART instatement however we have to roll out certain improvements for the Bluetooth to work immaculately with our PIC16F877A MCU. How about we characterize the arrangement bits and start with the Bluetooth instatement work.

Instating Bluetooth:

Practically all the Bluetooth modules in the market work at a baud pace of 9600, it is imperative to set your baud rate same as that of Bluetooth modules working baud rate, here we set SPBRG=129 since we are working at 20Mhz clock recurrence with 9600 as baud rate. Subsequently the above instatement will work just for Bluetooth modules working at 9600 baud rate. It is likewise required to have the rapid baud rate bit BRGH empowered. This will help in setting a precise baud rate.

```
//******Initialize Bluetooth using USART********//

void Initialize_Bluetooth()

{

  //Set the pins of RX and TX//

  TRISC6=1;

  TRISC7=1;
```

```
//Set the baud rate using the look up table in da-
tasheet(pg114)//

BRGH=1;   //Always use high speed baud rate with
Bluetooth else it wont work

SPBRG =129;

//Turn on Asyc. Serial Port//

SYNC=0;

SPEN=1;

//Set 8-bit reception and transmission

RX9=0;

TX9=0;

//Enable transmission and reception//

 TXEN=1;

 CREN=1;

//Enable global and ph. interrupts//

GIE = 1;
```

```
    PEIE= 1;

    //Enable interrupts for Tx. and Rx.//

    RCIE=1;

    TXIE=1;

}

//___________BT initialized_____________//
```

On the off chance that you have a BT module which works at an alternate baud rate, at that point you can allude the look into table beneath to discover your incentive for the SPBRG.

BAUD RATE (K)	Fosc = 20 MHz			Fosc = 16 MHz			Fosc = 10 MHz		
	KBAUD	% ERROR	SPBRG value (decimal)	KBAUD	% ERROR	SPBRG value (decimal)	KBAUD	% ERROR	SPBRG value (decimal)
0.3	-	-	-	-	-	-	-	-	-
1.2	-	-	-	-	-	-	-	-	-
2.4	-	-	-	-	-	-	2.441	1.71	255
9.6	9.615	0.16	129	9.615	0.16	103	9.615	0.16	64
19.2	19.231	0.16	64	19.231	0.16	51	19.531	1.72	31
28.8	29.070	0.94	42	29.412	2.13	33	28.409	1.36	21
33.6	33.784	0.55	36	33.333	0.79	29	32.895	2.10	18
57.6	59.524	3.34	20	58.824	2.13	16	56.818	1.36	10
HIGH	4.883	-	255	3.906	-	255	2.441	-	255
LOW	1250.000	-	0	1000.000	-	0	625.000	-	0

BAUD RATE (K)	Fosc = 4 MHz			Fosc = 3.6864 MHz		
	KBAUD	% ERROR	SPBRG value (decimal)	KBAUD	% ERROR	SPBRG value (decimal)
0.3	-	-	-	-	-	-
1.2	1.202	0.17	207	1.2	0	191
2.4	2.404	0.17	103	2.4	0	95
9.6	9.615	0.16	25	9.6	0	23
19.2	19.231	0.16	12	19.2	0	11
28.8	27.798	3.55	8	28.8	0	7
33.6	35.714	6.29	6	32.9	2.04	6
57.6	62.500	8.51	3	57.6	0	3
HIGH	0.977	-	255	0.9	-	255
LOW	250.000	-	0	230.4	-	0

Stacking information into Bluetooth:

When the capacity is instated we have three capacities in our program to send and get information from Bluetooth. Not at all like UART we have not many interesting points here before we can transmit or get information. The Bluetooth module has a Transmit and Receive cushion inside it, the information sent to it will be put away in the Tx support. This information won't be communicated (sent on air) except if a carriage return is sent to the module. Subsequently so as to transmit information we need to stack the Rx cradle of BT and afterward communicate it utilizing carriage return.

The above working can be handily accomplished by utilizing the accompanying capacities. The beneath capacity can be utilized when we require to stack just one character into the Rx cradle. We load the information into the TXREG register and hold up till it is prepared with a money order on the banner TXIF and TRMT by utilizing while circles.

```
//Function to load the Bluetooth Rx. buffer with one char.//

void BT_load_char(char byte)

{

    TXREG = byte;

    while(!TXIF);

    while(!TRMT);

}

//End of function//
```

Underneath work is utilized to stack a string into the Rx cradle of the Bluetooth module. The string is part into characters along with each character is sent to the BT_load_char() work.

```
//Function to Load Bluetooth Rx. buffer with string//

void BT_load_string(char* string)

{

    while(*string)

    BT_load_char(*string++);

}

//End of function/
```

Broadcasting information over Bluetooth:

Till now we have quite recently transmitted data into the Rx support of the HC-05 module. Presently we should educate it to communicate the information over air by utilizing this capacity.

```
//Function to broadcast data from RX. buffer//

void broadcast_BT()
```

```
{

  TXREG = 13;

  __delay_ms(500);

}

//End of function//
```

In this capacity we send a worth 13 into the TXREG register. This worth 13 is only the decimal identical for carriage (allude ASCII graph). At that point a little deferral is made for the telecaster to begin.

Perusing information from Bluetooth:

Like UART, the underneath work is used to peruse information from the Bluetooth

```
//Function to get a char from Rx.buffer of BT//

char BT_get_char(void)

{

    if(OERR) // check for over run error

    {
```

```
    CREN = 0;

    CREN = 1; //Reset CREN

  }

  if(RCIF==1) //if the user has sent a char return the
char (ASCII value)

  {

  while(!RCIF);

  return RCREG;

  }

  else //if user has sent no message return 0

    return 0;

}

//End of function/
```

In case the client has sent an information, this capacity will restore that specific information which can be spared in a variable and handled. In the event that the client has not sent anything the capacity will bring zero back.

Principle work:

We have utilized all the above clarified works inside or principle work. We send some initial message and afterward trust that the client will send a few qualities dependent on which we flip the RED drove light associated with the RB3 nail to our Perfboard.

```
void main(void)

{

    //Scope variable declarations//

    int get_value;

    //End of variable declaration//

    //I/O Declarations//

    TRISB3=0;

    //End of I/O declaration//

    Initialize_Bluetooth(); //lets get our bluetooth
ready for action

    //Show some introductory message once on
```

```
power up//

  BT_load_string("Bluetooth          Initialized          and
Ready");

  broadcast_BT();

  BT_load_string("Press 1 to turn ON LED");

  broadcast_BT();

  BT_load_string("Press 0 to turn OFF LED");

  broadcast_BT();

  //End of message//

  while(1) //The infinite lop

  {

  get_value = BT_get_char(); //Read the char. re-
ceived via BT

  //If we receive a '0'//

    if(get_value=='0')

    {
```

```c
        RB3=0;

        BT_load_string("LED turned OFF");

        broadcast_BT();

    }

  //If we receive a '1'//

    if(get_value=='1')

    {

        RB3=1;

        BT_load_string("LED turned ON");

        broadcast_BT();

    }

  }

}
```

Check the Full Program in the Code Section Below.

Circuit Diagram and Hardware Setup:

Circuit associations for this venture is basic, we basically require to manage up the Bluetooth module and interface the Tx to the 26th pin of PIC and Rx to the 25th pin of PIC as appeared in the circuit outline beneath:

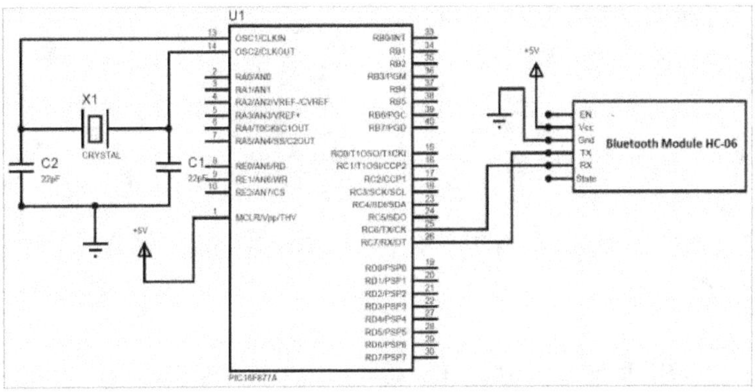

Presently let us continue to the equipment. When the association is done it should look something like this.

Controlling LED utilizing Bluetooth Mobile Application:

Presently let us prepare our Android application. Install the application called Bluetooth Terminal from the App store otherwise utilize this connection. When the application is downloaded and introduced, turn on your PIC perf board which we are utilizing since starting. The little LED light on your Bluetooth Module ought to blaze to demonstrate that it is fueled on and is effectively searching for a telephone to build up an association.

Presently get into the Bluetooth Settings of your telephone and quest for new Bluetooth gadget you ought to have the option to see the name HC-05 or HC-06 dependent on your module. I am utilizing HC-06 subsequently my telephone shows the accompanying showcase. At that point have a go at paring with it and it will request a secret phrase. Enter the secret phrase as 1234 (for some it may be 0000) and click OK as demonstrated as follows.

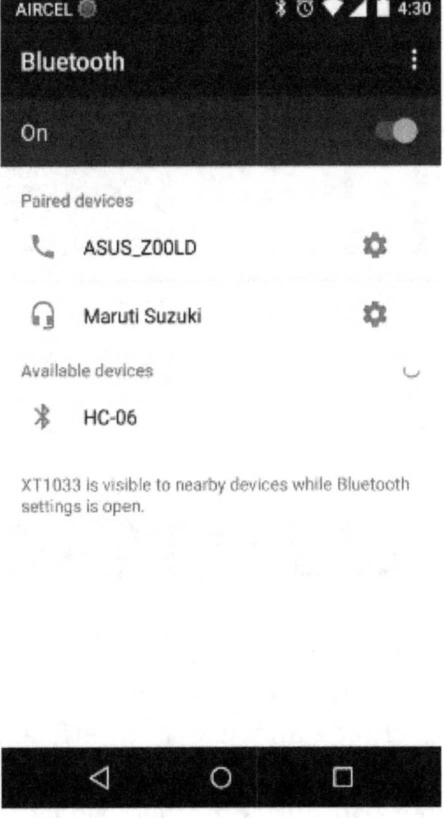

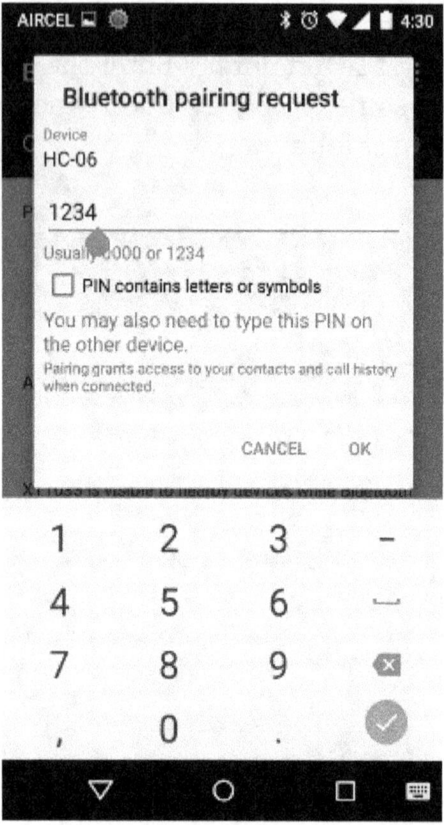

After the paring is fruitful, open the Bluetooth Terminal application that we just introduced. Get into the settings choice and select "Interface a gadget – Secure" as demonstrated as follows. This will open a pop box where all our combined gadgets will be recorded as demonstrated as follows. Select the HC-05 or HC-06 module.

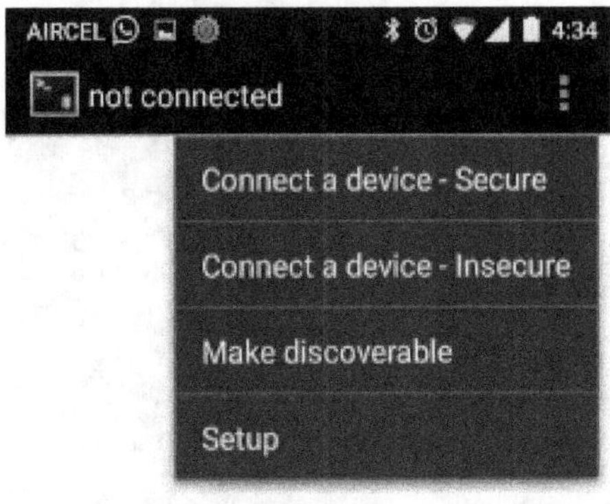
AIRCEL 4:34
not connected
Connect a device - Secure
Connect a device - Insecure
Make discoverable
Setup

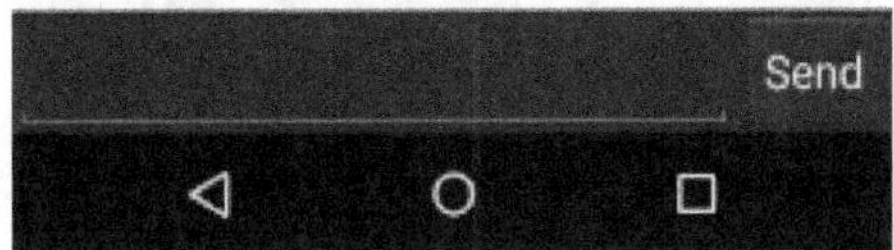
Send

When the association is set up, the light on the Bluetooth module which was blazing so far more likely than not become consistent to demonstrate that it has effectively associated with your portable. Furthermore, we must get the early on message from our Program like demonstrated as follows.

Presently press '1' to turn on the LED light and press '0' to kill the light. Your portable screen will look like this demonstrated as follows.

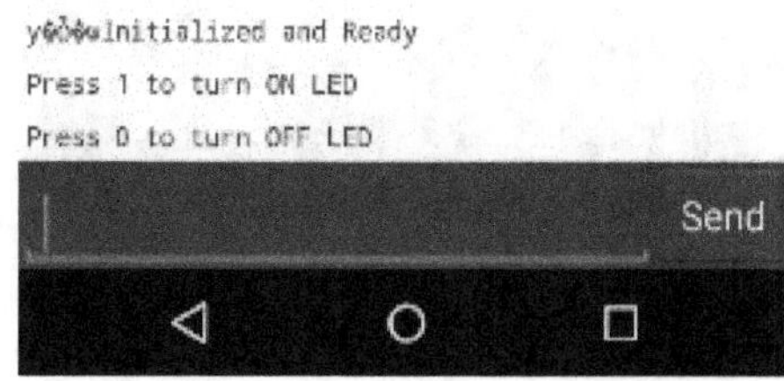

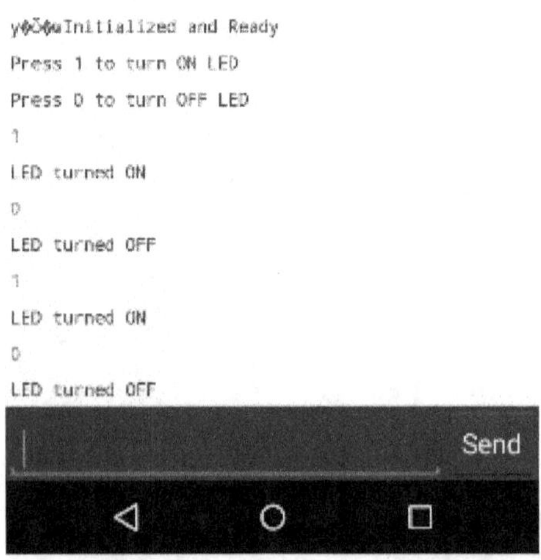

So that is it folks, we have find How to Interface Bluetooth module to our PIC microcontroller, presently with the guide of this we can attempt remote undertakings. There are loads of tasks which utilizes Bluetooth, you can attempt them or think of your own Idea and do share them in the remark segment. Additionally check our past venture with Bluetooth terminal application and HC-05 like Smart Phone Controlled Home Automation Using Arduino along with Smart Phone Controlled Digital Code Lock utilizing Arduino.

Expectation, this instructional exercise helped you! In the event that you stalled out some place, mercifully utilize the remark area.

Code

```
// CONFIG
#pragma config FOSC = HS     // Oscillator Selection bits (HS oscillator)
#pragma config WDTE = OFF      // Watchdog Timer Enable bit (WDT disabled)
#pragma config PWRTE = OFF     // Power-up Timer Enable bit (PWRT enabled)
#pragma config BOREN = OFF     // Brown-out Reset Enable bit (BOR enabled)
#pragma config LVP = OFF       // Low-Voltage (Single-Supply) In-Circuit Serial Programming Enable bit (RB3 is digital I/O, HV on MCLR must be used for programming)
#pragma config CPD = OFF    // Data EEPROM Memory Code Protection bit (Data EEPROM code protection off)
#pragma config WRT = OFF    // Flash Program Memory Write Enable bits (Write protection off; all program memory may be written to by EECON control)
#pragma config CP = OFF    // Flash Program Memory Code Protection bit (Code protection off)
//End of CONFIG registers
```

```c
#define _XTAL_FREQ 20000000
#include<xc.h>

//******Initialize Bluetooth using USART********//
void Initialize_Bluetooth()
{
 //Set the pins of RX and TX//
  TRISC6=1;
  TRISC7=1;


  //Set the baud rate using the look up table in da-
tasheet(pg114)//
   BRGH=1;    //Always use high speed baud rate with
Bluetooth else it wont work
  SPBRG =129;


   //Turn on Asyc. Serial Port//
  SYNC=0;
  SPEN=1;


   //Set 8-bit reception and transmission
  RX9=0;
  TX9=0;

  //Enable transmission and reception//
  TXEN=1;
  CREN=1;

   //Enable global and ph. interrupts//
```

```c
  GIE = 1;
  PEIE= 1;


    //Enable interrupts for Tx. and Rx.//
  RCIE=1;
  TXIE=1;
}
//___________BT initialized_____________//

//Function to load the Bluetooth Rx. buffer with one
char.//
void BT_load_char(char byte)
{
  TXREG = byte;
  while(!TXIF);
  while(!TRMT);
}
//End of function//

//Function to Load Bluetooth Rx. buffer with string//
void BT_load_string(char* string)
{
  while(*string)
  BT_load_char(*string++);
}
//End of function//

//Function to broadcast data from RX. buffer//
void broadcast_BT()
{
 TXREG = 13;
```

```c
  __delay_ms(500);
}
//End of function//

//Function to get a char from Rx.buffer of BT//
char BT_get_char(void)
{
  if(OERR) // check for over run error
  {
    CREN = 0;
    CREN = 1; //Reset CREN
  }


    if(RCIF==1) //if the user has sent a char return the char (ASCII value)
  {
  while(!RCIF);
  return RCREG;
  }
  else //if user has sent no message return 0
    return 0;
}
//End of function/

void main(void)
{
  //Scope variable declarations//
  int get_value;
  //End of variable declaration//
```

```c
  //I/O Declarations//
 TRISB3=0;
 //End of I/O declaration//


  Initialize_Bluetooth(); //lets get our bluetooth
ready for action


  //Show some introductory message once on power
up//
 BT_load_string("Bluetooth Initialized and Ready");
 broadcast_BT();
 BT_load_string("Press 1 to turn ON LED");
 broadcast_BT();
 BT_load_string("Press 0 to turn OFF LED");
 broadcast_BT();
 //End of message//


  while(1) //The infinite lop
 {


  get_value = BT_get_char(); //Read the char. re-
ceived via BT


  //If we receive a '0'//
  if(get_value=='0')
  {
    RB3=0;
```

```c
    BT_load_string("LED turned OFF");
    broadcast_BT();
  }


  //If we receive a '1'//
  if(get_value=='1')
   {
    RB3=1;
    BT_load_string("LED turned ON");
    broadcast_BT();
   }
 }
}
```

◆ ◆ ◆

4. UART COMMUNICATION UTILIZING PIC MICROCONTROLLER

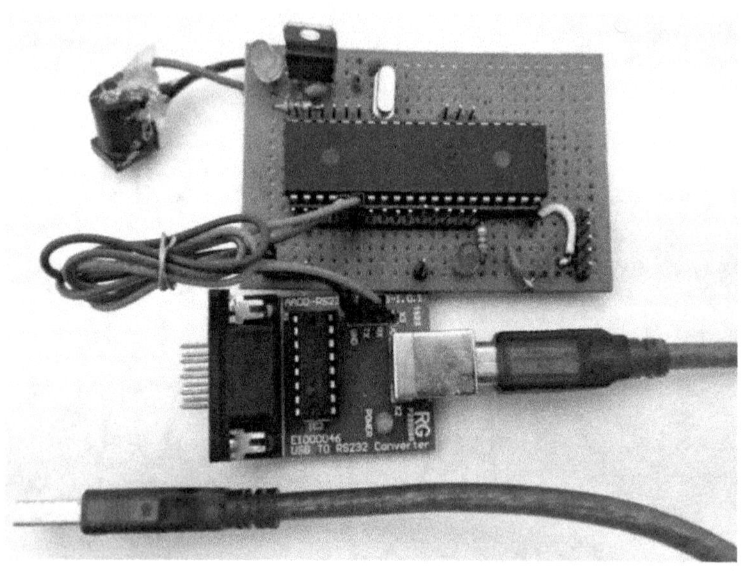

In this instructional exercise we figure out how to Enable UART correspondence with PIC Microcontroller and how to move information to and from your Computer. Up until this point, we have secured every single essential module like ADC, Timers, PWM and furthermore have figured out how to interface LCDs and 7-Segment shows. Presently, we will outfit our self with another specialized instrument called UART which generally utilized in the greater part of the Microcontroller ventures. Check here our total PIC Microcontroller Tutorials utilizing MPLAB along with XC8.

Here we have utilized PIC16F877A MCU, it has a module called "Addressable Universal Synchronous Asynchronous Receiver and Transmitter" instantly known as USART. USART is a two wire correspondence framework in which the information stream sequentially. USART is additionally a full-duplex correspondence, implies you can send and get information simultaneously which can be utilized to speak with fringe gadgets, for example, CRT terminals along with PCs.

The USART can be designed in the accompanying modes:

- Offbeat (full-duplex)

- Coordinated – Master (half-duplex)

- Coordinated – Slave (half-duplex)

There are likewise two unique modes to be specific the 8-piece and 9-piece mode, in this instructional exercise we will arrange the USART module to work in Asynchronous mode with 8-piece correspondence framework, since it is the most utilized sort of correspondence. As it is nonconcurrent it doesn't have to impart clock sign alongside the information signals. UART utilizes 2 information lines for sending (Tx) and getting (Rx) information. The ground of the 2 gadgets ought to likewise be made normal. This kind of correspondence doesn't share a typical clock henceforth a shared opinion is significant for the framework to work.

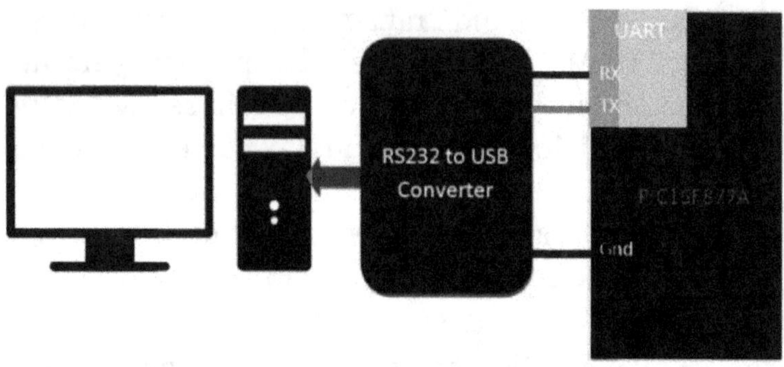

Toward the finish of this instructional exercise you will be capable build up a correspondence (UART) between your PC along with your PIC Microcontroller and flip a LED on the PIC board from your PC. The status of the Light Emitting Diode will be sent to your PC from the PIC MCU. We will test the yield utilizing Hyper Terminal in PC.

Necessities:

Equipment:

- PIC16F877A Perf Board

- RS232 to USB converter Module

- PC

- PICkit 3 Programmer

Programming:

- MPLABX

- HyperTerminal

A RS232 to USB converter is required to change over the sequential information into PC coherent structure. There are approaches to plan your own circuit as against to purchasing your own module yet they are not solid as they are oppressed clamor. The one which we are utilizing is demonstrated as follows

Note: Each RS232 to Universal Serial Bus converter would require an exceptional driver to be introduced; the majority of them must get introduced consequently when you plug in the gadget. However, in case it doesn't unwind!!! Utilize the remark segment and I will get you out.

Programming PIC Microcontroller for UART Communication:

Like all modules (ADC, Timer, PWM) we ought to likewise introduce our USART module of our PIC16F877A MCU and train it to work in UART 8-piece correspondence mode. How about we characterize the design bits and start with the UART introduction work.

Instating the UART module of the PIC Microcontroller:

The Tx and Rx pins are truly present at the pins RC6 and RC7. As per datasheet how about we pronounce TX as yield and RX as information.

```
//****Setting I/O pins for UART****//

TRISC6 = 0; // TX Pin set as output

TRISC7 = 1; // RX Pin set as input

//__________I/O pins set __________//
```

Presently the baud rate must be set. The baud rate is

the rate at which data is moved in a correspondence channel. This can be one of the many default esteems, however in this program we are utilizing 9600 since its the most utilized baud rate.

```
/**Initialize SPBRG register for required

   baud rate and set BRGH for fast baud_rate**/

SPBRG = ((_XTAL_FREQ/16)/Baud_rate) - 1;

BRGH = 1; // for high baud_rate

//__________End of baud_rate setting__________//
```

The estimation of the baud rate must be set utilizing the register SPBRG, the worth relies upon the estimation of the External precious stone recurrence, the formulae to figure the baud rate is demonstrated as follows:

```
SPBRG = ( ( _XTAL_FREQ/16 ) / Baud_rate) – 1;
```

The bit BRGH must be made high to empower rapid piece rate. As indicated by datasheet (page 13) it is constantly worthwhile to empower it, as it can wipe out blunders during correspondence.

As said before we will be working in Asynchronous

mode, henceforth the bit SYNC ought to be made zero and bit SPEM must be made high to empower sequential pins (TRISC6 and TRICSC5)

```
//****Enable Asynchronous serial port*******//

   SYNC = 0;  // Asynchronous

   SPEN = 1;  // Enable serial port pins

   //_____Asynchronous    serial    port    en-
abled________//
```

In this instructional exercise we will be both sending and getting information among MCU and PC henceforth we require to empower both TXEN and CREN bits.

```
//**Lets prepare for transmission & reception**//

   TXEN = 1;  // enable transmission

   CREN = 1;  // enable reception

   //__UART module up and ready for transmission
and reception__//
```

The bits TX9 and RX9 must be caused zero so we to

work in 8-piece mode. In the event that there must be high unwavering quality should be set up, at that point 9-piece mode can be chosen.

```
//**Select 8-bit mode**//

    TX9  = 0;  // 8-bit reception selected

    RX9  = 0;  // 8-bit reception mode selected

    //__8-bit mode selected__//
```

With this we complete our instatement arrangement. Presently the Module is designed as UART and is prepared for activity.

Transmitting information utilizing UART:

The beneath capacity can be used to transmit information through the UART module:

```
//**Function to send one byte of date to UART**//

void UART_send_char(char bt)

{

    while(!TXIF); //hold the program till TX buffer is
```

```
free

    TXREG = bt; //Load the transmitter buffer with
the received value


}


//______________End            of            func-
tion________________//
```

When the module is instated whatever worth is stacked into the register TXREG will be transmitted across UART, however transmission may cover. Subsequently we must consistently check for the Transmission Interrupt banner TXIF. Just if this bit is low we can continue with the following piece for transmission else we should trust that this banner will get low.

Be that as it may, above capacity can be utilized uniquely to send just a single byte of information, to send a total a string the beneath capacity ought to be utilized

```
//**Function to convert string to byte**//

void UART_send_string(char* st_pt)

{
```

```
    while(*st_pt) //if there is a char

     UART_send_char(*st_pt++); //process it as a
byte data


}


//____________End of function____________//
```

This capacity may be somewhat precarious to comprehend since it has pointers, yet trust me pointers are magnificent and they make programming all the more simple and this is one genuine case of the equivalent.

As you can view we have again called the UART_send_char() yet now inside the while circle. We have part the string into singular characters, each time this capacity is called, one scorch will be sent to the TXREG and it will get transmitted.

Getting information utilizing UART:

The accompanying capacity can be used to get information from the UART module:

```
//**Function to get one byte of date from UART**//

char UART_get_char()
```

```
{

    if(OERR) // check for Error

    {

        CREN = 0; //If error -> Reset

        CREN = 1; //If error -> Reset

    }

    while(!RCIF); // hold the program till RX buffer is free

    return RCREG; //receive the value and send it to main function

}

//_______________End          of          func-
tion________________//
```

At the point when an information is gotten by the UART module it gets it and hides away up in the RCREG register. We can just exchange the incentive to any factor and use it. Be that as it may, there may be cover mistake or the client may be sending information constantly and we have not yet moved them to a variable.

Considering all the Receive banner piece RCIF acts the hero. This bit will go low at whatever point an information is gotten and isn't yet prepared. Thus we use it in the while circle making a postponement to hold the program till we manage that esteem.

Flipping LED utilizing the UART module of PIC Microcontroller:

Presently let us go to the last piece of the Program, the void main(void) work, where we will flip a LED through the PC utilizing the UART correspondence among PIC and PC.

At the point when we send a character "1" (from PC) the Light Emitting Diode will be turned ON along with the status message "RED LED - > ON" will be sent back (from PIC MCU) to the PC.

Correspondingly we send a character "0" (from PC) the LED will be killed and the status message "RED LED - > OFF" will be sent back (from PIC MCU) to the PC.

```
while(1) //Infinite loop

  {

    get_value = UART_get_char();

      if(get_value == '1') //If the user sends "1"
```

```
    {

        RB3 = 1; //Turn on LED

        UART_send_string("RED LED -> ON"); //Send
notification to the computer

        UART_send_char(10);//ASCII  value  10  is
used for carriage return (to print in new line)

    }

    if(get_value == '0') //If the user sends "0"

    {

        RB3 = 0; //Turn off LED

        UART_send_string("RED -> OFF"); //Send no-
tification to the computer

        UART_send_char(10);//ASCII  value  10  is
used for carriage return (to print in new line)

    }

  }
```

Reproducing our program:

As normal we should recreate our program utilizing proteus and see whether it fills in true to form.

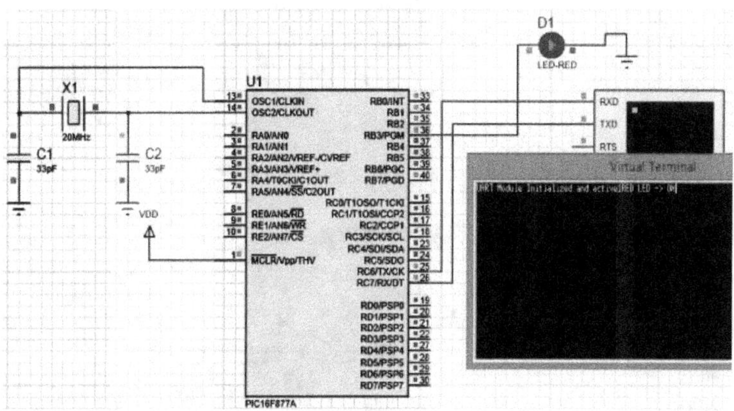

The above picture shows a virtual terminal where 1 it shows an invite message along with status of the Light Emitting Diode. The Red Color LED can be seen to be associated with the pin RB3.

Equipment Setup and Testing the yield:

The association for this circuit is extremely straight-forward, we utilize our PIC Perf board and simply interface the three wires to RS232 to Universal Serial Bus converter and associate the module to our PC utilizing USB information link as demonstrated as follows.

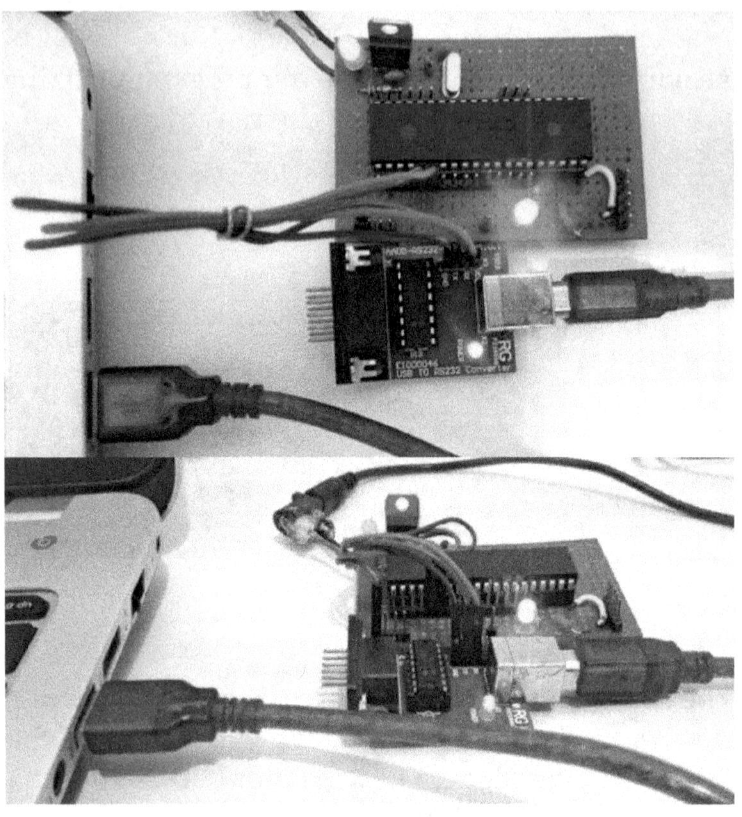

Next we introduce the Hyper Terminal Application (install it from here) along with open it up. It should show like this

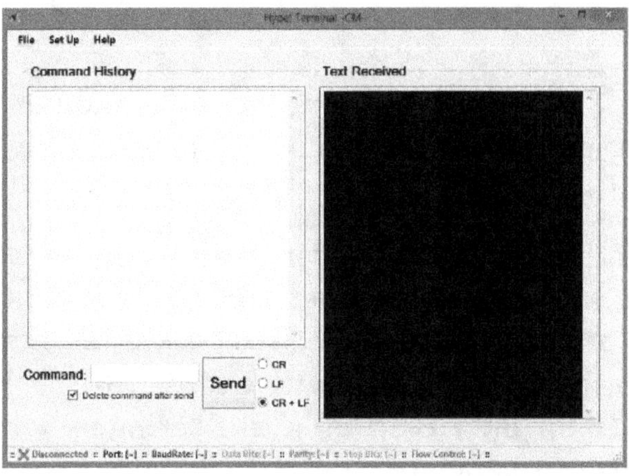

Presently open Device Manager on your PC and check which Com port your module is associated with, mine is associated with COM port 17 as demonstrated as follows

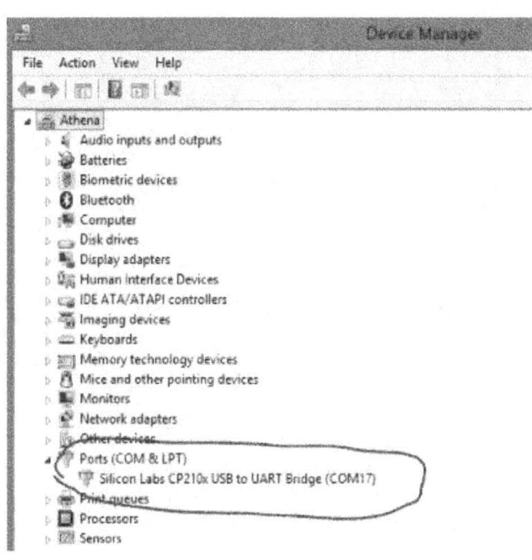

Note: The COM port name for your module may change as indicated by your merchant, it's anything but an issue.

Presently return to Hyper Terminal Application along with explore to Set Up - > Port Configuration otherwise press Alt+C, to get the accompanying spring up box along with choose the ideal port (COM17 for my situation) in the spring up window and snap on associate.

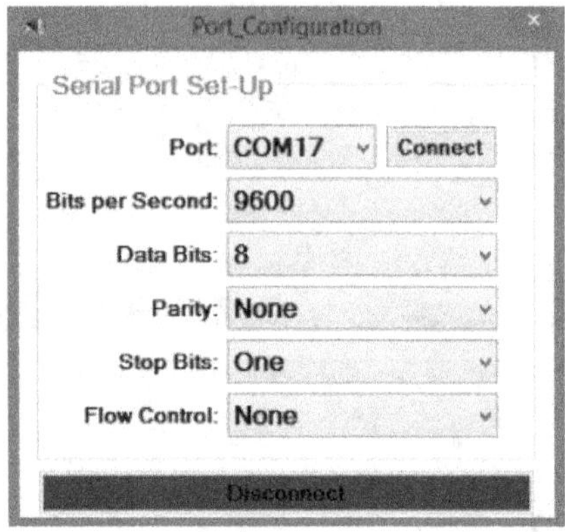

When the association is set up turn on your PIC perf board along with you should view like this beneath

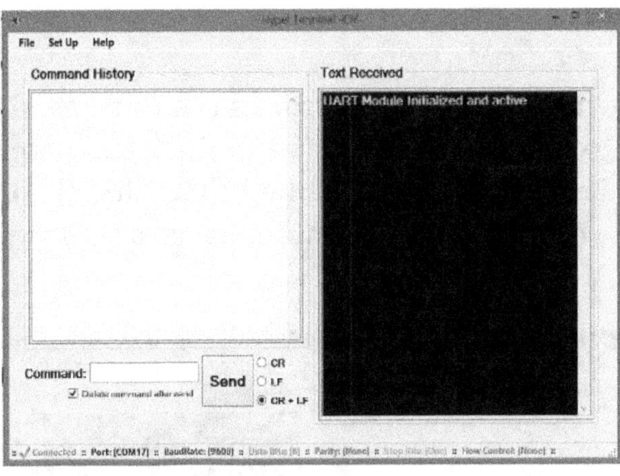

Keep your cursor in the Command Window along with enter 1 at that point press enter. The LED will be turned on along with the status will be shown as demonstrated as follows.

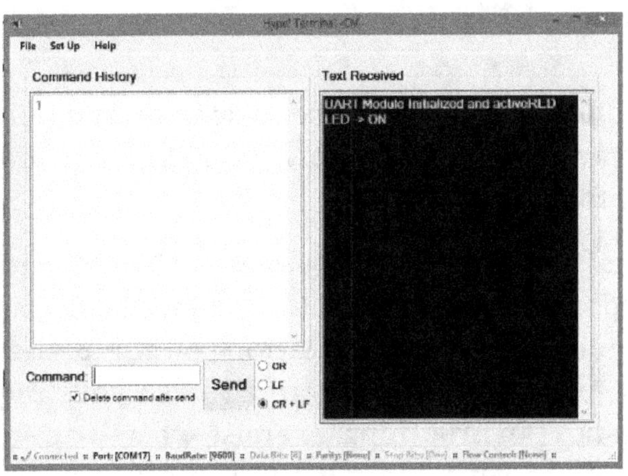

Same way , keep your cursor in the Command Window along with enter 0 at that point press enter. The Light Emitting Diode will be killed along with the status will be shown as demonstrated as follows.

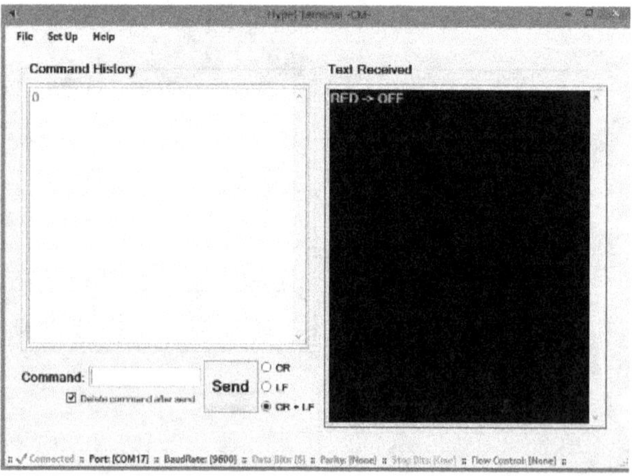

The following are given the total code and point by point, which will show how the LED reacts progressively for "1" and "0".

That is it folks, we have interfaced PIC UART with our PC and moved the information to flip the LED utilizing Hyper terminal. Expectation you comprehended, if not, utilize the remark area to ask your inquiry. In our next instructional exercise we will again utilize UART however make it all the more intriguing by utilizing a Bluetooth module and communicate the information over air.

Additionally check UART Communication among 2 ATmega8 Microcontrollers and UART correspondence among ATmega8 along with Arduino Uno.

Code

```
// CONFIG
#pragma config FOSC = HS      // Oscillator Selection bits (HS oscillator)
#pragma config WDTE = OFF      // Watchdog Timer Enable bit (WDT disabled)
#pragma config PWRTE = OFF      // Power-up Timer Enable bit (PWRT enabled)
#pragma config BOREN = ON      // Brown-out Reset Enable bit (BOR enabled)
#pragma config LVP = OFF      // Low-Voltage (Single-Supply) In-Circuit Serial Programming Enable bit (RB3 is digital I/O, HV on MCLR must be used for programming)
#pragma config CPD = OFF    // Data EEPROM Memory Code Protection bit (Data EEPROM code protection off)
#pragma config WRT = OFF     // Flash Program Memory Write Enable bits (Write protection off; all program memory may be written to by EECON control)
#pragma config CP = OFF     // Flash Program Memory Code Protection bit (Code protection off)
// End of configuration
```

```c
#include <xc.h>
#define _XTAL_FREQ 20000000
#define Baud_rate 9600

//***Initializing UART module for PIC16F877A***//
void Initialize_UART(void)
{
  //****Setting I/O pins for UART****//
  TRISC6 = 0; // TX Pin set as output
  TRISC7 = 1; // RX Pin set as input
  //_________I/O pins set ___________//


  /**Initialize SPBRG register for required
  baud rate and set BRGH for fast baud_rate**/
  SPBRG = ((_XTAL_FREQ/16)/Baud_rate) - 1;
  BRGH = 1; // for high baud_rate
  //_________End of baud_rate setting_________//


  //****Enable Asynchronous serial port*******//
  SYNC = 0;  // Asynchronous
  SPEN = 1;  // Enable serial port pins
  //_____Asynchronous serial port enabled________//

  //**Lets prepare for transmission & reception**//
  TXEN = 1;  // enable transmission
  CREN = 1;  // enable reception
  //__UART module up and ready for transmission and
reception__//


  //**Select 8-bit mode**//
```

```
  TX9  = 0;  // 8-bit reception selected
  RX9  = 0;  // 8-bit reception mode selected
  //__8-bit mode selected__//
}
//________UART module Initialized__________//

//**Function to send one byte of date to UART**//
void UART_send_char(char bt)
{
   while(!TXIF);  // hold the program till TX buffer is
free
   TXREG = bt; //Load the transmitter buffer with the
received value
}
//_____________End of function________________//

//**Function to get one byte of date from UART**//
char UART_get_char()
{
  if(OERR) // check for Error
  {
    CREN = 0; //If error -> Reset
    CREN = 1; //If error -> Reset
  }


    while(!RCIF);  // hold the program till RX buffer is
free


    return RCREG; //receive the value and send it to
main function
```

```c
}
//________________End of function________________//

//**Function to convert string to byte**//
void UART_send_string(char* st_pt)
{
  while(*st_pt) //if there is a char
    UART_send_char(*st_pt++); //process it as a byte
data
}
//____________End of function______________//

// *********START of Main Function*************//
void main(void)
{
  int get_value;

    TRISB = 0x00; //Initialize PortB as output
  Initialize_UART();  //Initialize UART module

    UART_send_string("UART Module Initialized and
active");  // Introductory Text

    while(1) //Infinite loop
  {
  get_value = UART_get_char();

      if(get_value == '1') //If the user sends "1"
    {
```

```c
    RB3 = 1; //Turn on LED
    UART_send_string("RED LED -> ON"); //Send notification to the computer
    UART_send_char(10);//ASCII value 10 is used for carriage return (to print in new line)
    }


        if(get_value == '0') //If the user sends "0"
    {
    RB3 = 0; //Turn off LED
    UART_send_string("RED -> OFF"); //Send notification to the computer
    UART_send_char(10);//ASCII value 10 is used for carriage return (to print in new line)
    }


    }
}
//**********END of Main Function*************//
```

◆ ◆ ◆

5. INTERFACING SERVO MOTOR WITH PIC MICROCONTROLLER UTILIZING MPLAB AND XC8

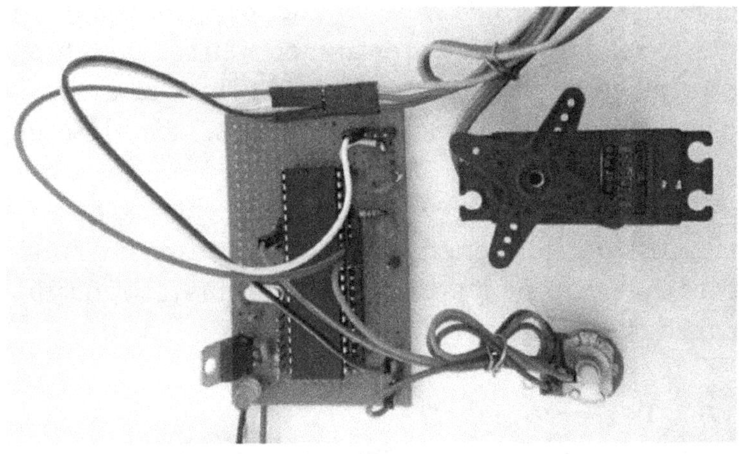

This is our eleventh instructional exercise of Learning PIC microcontrollers utilizing MPLAB and XC8. In this instructional exercise we will figure out How to control Servo Motor with PIC Microcontroller. In case you have just worked with Servo engines you can skirt the primary portion of this instructional exercise however in case you are new to servo engine itself, in this point keep perusing.

Till now, we have secured numerous fundamental instructional exercises like LED flickering with PIC, Timers in PIC, interfacing LCD, interfacing 7-section, ADC utilizing PIC and so forth. In case you are an outright tenderfoot, in this point please visit the total rundown of PIC instructional exercises here and begin learning.

In our past instructional exercise we figured out how to produce PWM signals utilizing PIC Microcontroller, the signs were created dependent on the worth read from the potentiometer. In case you have seen all projects, at that point, Congratulations you have just coded for a Servo engine too. Indeed, Servo engines react to the PWM signals (which we make utilizing clocks here) we will realize why and how in this instructional exercise. We will reenact and fabricate the equipment arrangement for this task and you can locate the itemized toward.

What is a Servo Motor?
A Servo Motor is a kind of actuator (for the most part roundabout) that permits precise control. There are numerous sorts of Servo engines accessible yet in this instructional exercise let us focus on the leisure activity servo engines demonstrated as follows.

Pastime servos are a famous in light in case they are the cheap technique for movement control. They give an off-the-rack answer for the greater part of the R/C and automated specialist's needs. They additionally dispense with the require to specially craft a control framework for every application.

The greater part of the leisure activity servo engines have a rotational heavenly attendant of 0-180° yet you can likewise get 360° servo engine in case you're intrigued. This instructional exercise utilizes a 0-180° servo engine. There are 2 kinds of Servo engines dependent on the rigging, 1 is the Plastic Gear Servo Motor along with the other is Metal Gear Servo Motor. Metal apparatus is utilized in places where the engine is exposed to more mileage, however it comes just at a significant expense.

Servo engines are appraised in kg/cm (kilogram per

centimeter) most interest servo engines are evaluated at 3kg/cm otherwise 6kg/cm otherwise 12kg/cm. This kg/cm reveals to you how much weight your servo engine can lift at a specific separation. For instance: A 6kg/cm Servo engine ought to have the option to lift 6kg if the heap is suspended 1cm away from the engines shaft, the more noteworthy the separation the lesser the weight conveying limit. Learn here the Basics of Servo engine.

Interfacing Servo Motors with Microcontrollers:

Interfacing pastime Servo engines with MCU is simple. Servos have three wires coming out of them. Out of which two will be utilized for Supply (positive and negative) and one will be utilized for the sign that will be sent from the MCU. In this instructional exercise we will utilize a MG995 Metal Gear Servo Motor which is most ordinarily utilized for RC vehicles humanoid bots and so on. The image of MG995 is demonstrated as follows:

The shading coding of your servo engine may contrast henceforth check for your particular datasheet.

Every servo engine work straightforwardly with your +5V flexibly rails however we must be cautious on the measure of current the engine would expend, on the off chance that you are intending to utilize in excess of two servo engines an appropriate servo shield ought to be planned. In this instructional exercise we will essentially utilize one servo engine to tell the best way to program our PIC MCU to control the engine. Check beneath joins for interfacing Servo Motor with other Microcontroller:

- Servo engine interfacing with 8051 microcontroller

- Servo engine manage utilizing Arduino

- Raspberry Pi Servo Motor Tutorial

- Servo Motor with AVR Microcontroller

Programming Servo Motor with PICF877A PIC Microcontroller:

Before we can begin programming for the Servo engine we should comprehend what sort of sign is to be sent for controlling the Servo engine. We should program the MCU to impart PWM signs to the sign wire of the Servo engine. There is a control hardware inside the servo engine which peruses the obligation pattern of the PWM sign and positions the servo engines shaft in the particular spot as appeared in the image underneath

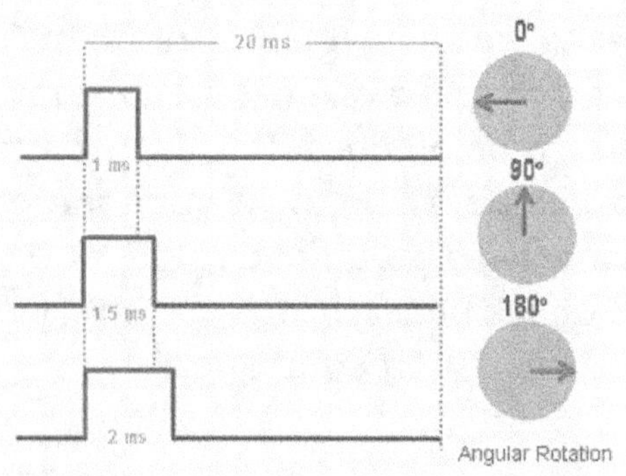

Every servo engine works on an alternate PWM frequencies (most normal recurrence is 50HZ which is utilized in this instructional exercise) so get the datasheet of your engine to check the on which PWM period your Servo engine works.

The subtleties on the PWM signal for our Tower professional MG995 is demonstrated as follows.

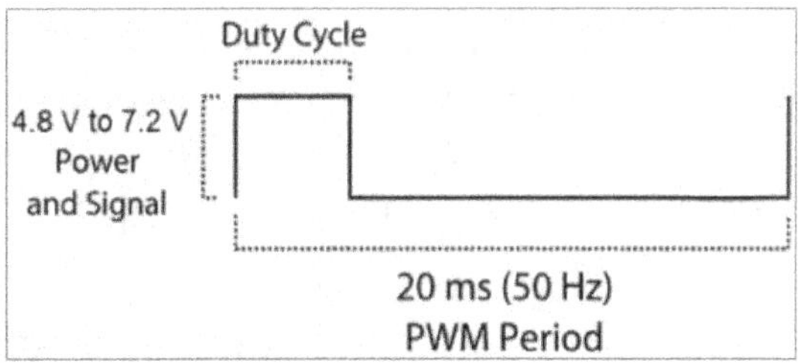

From this we can presume that our engine works with a PWM Period of 20ms (50Hz). So the recurrence of our PWM sign ought to be set to 50Hz. The recurrence of the PWM that we had set in our past instructional exercise was 5 KHz, utilizing a similar won't help us here.

In case, we have an issue here. The PIC16F877A can't create low recurrence PWM signals utilizing the CCP module. As per the datasheet the least conceivable worth that can be set for the PWM recurrence is 1.2 KHz. So we need to drop utilizing CCP module along with figure out how to do our own Pulse Width Modulation signals.

Consequently, in this instructional exercise we will utilize the clock module to create the PWM signals with 50Hz recurrence and fluctuate their obligation cycle to control the holy messenger of the servo engine. In the event that you are new to clocks or ADC with PIC please fall back to this instructional exercise, since I will avoid the greater part of the stuff since we have just secured them there.

We instate our Timer module with a prescaler of 32

and make it flood for each 1us. As per our information sheet the PWM ought to have a time of 20ms in particular. So our on schedule and off time together ought to be actually be equivalent to 20ms.

```
OPTION_REG = 0b00000100;  // Timer0 with ex-
ternal freq and 32 as prescaler

   TMR0=251;     // Load the time value for 1us de-
layValue can be between 0-256 only

   TMR0IE=1;    //Enable timer interrupt bit in PIE1
register

   GIE=1;       //Enable Global Interrupt

   PEIE=1;      //Enable the Peripheral Interrupt
```

So inside our interfere with routine capacity, we turn on the pin RB0 for the predefined time and turn it off for the reaming time (20ms – on_time). The estimation of the on time can be decided by utilizing the Potentiometer and ADC module. The hinder is demonstrated as follows.

```
oid interrupt timer_isr()

{
```

```
if(TMR0IF==1) // Timer has overflown

{

    TMR0 = 252;    /*Load the timer Value, (Note:
Timervalue is 101 instaed of 100 as the

            TImer0   needs   two   instruction
Cycles to start incrementing TMR0 */

    TMR0IF=0;    // Clear timer interrupt flag

    count++;

}

if(count >= on_time)

{

    RB0=1; // complement the value for blinking
the LEDs

}

if(count >= (on_time+(200-on_time)))

{

    RB0=0;
```

```
    count=0;

  }

}
```

Inside our while circle we simply read the estimation of potentiometer by utilizing the ADC module and update the on time of the PWM utilizing the read esteem.

```
while(1)

  {

    pot_value = (ADC_Read(4))*0.039;

    on_time = (170-pot_value);

  }
```

In this way we have made a PWM signal who's Period is 20ms and has a variable obligation cycle which can be set utilizing a Potentiometer. Complete Code has been given beneath in code segment.

Presently, we should confirm the yield utilizing proteus recreation and continue to our equipment.

Circuit Diagram:

On the off chance that you have just gone over the PWM instructional exercise, at that point the schematics of this instructional exercise will be same with the exception of which we will include a servo engine instead of the LED light.

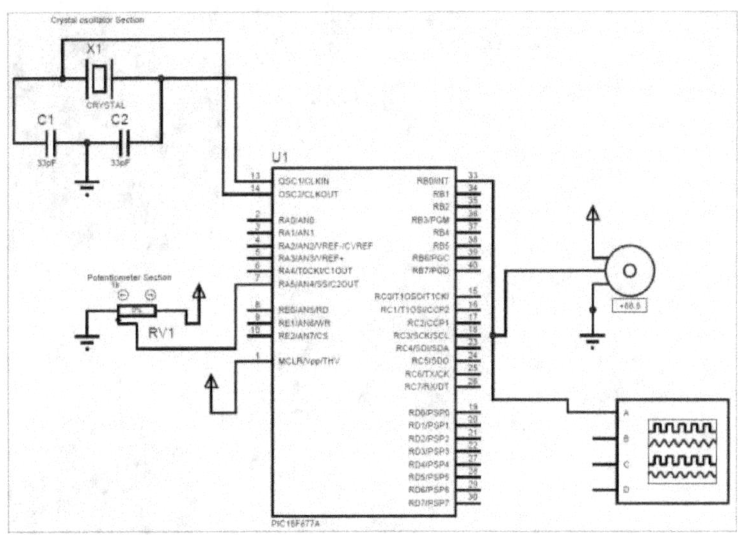

Recreation and Hardware Setup:

With the assistance of Proteus recreation we can confirm the PWM signal utilizing an oscilloscope and furthermore check the pivoting heavenly attendant of the Servo engine. Hardly any previews of the recreation is demonstrated as follows, where the turning blessed messenger of the servo engine and PWM obligation cycle can be seen to get changed dependent on the potentiometer.

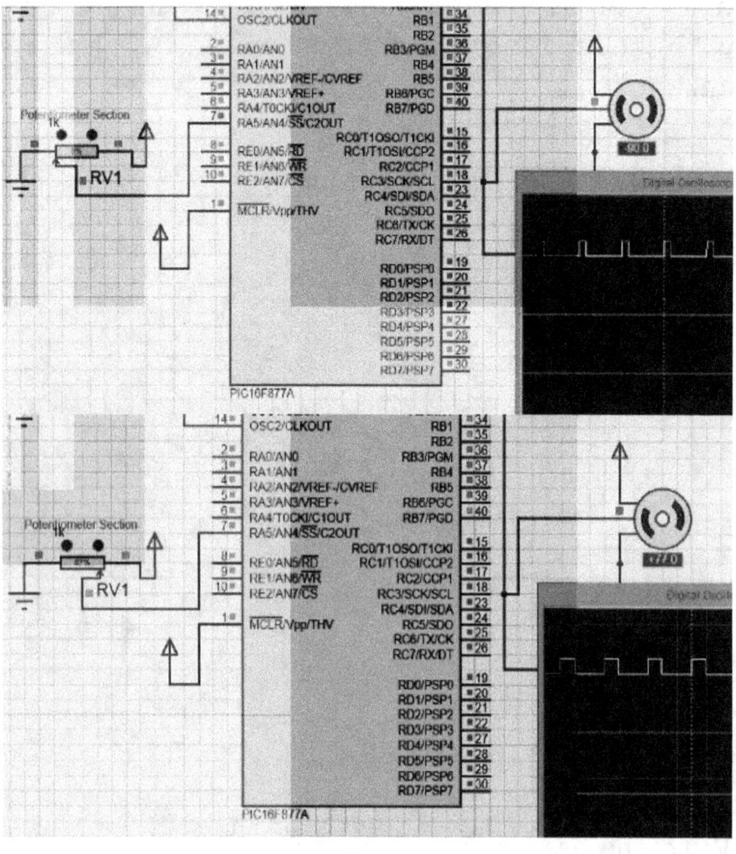

As should be obvious the servo pivot heavenly attendant gets changed dependent on the potentiometer esteem. Presently let us continue to our equipment arrangement.

In the equipment arrangement we have recently expelled the LED board and included the Servo engine as appeared in the schematics above.

The equipment is appeared in the image beneath:

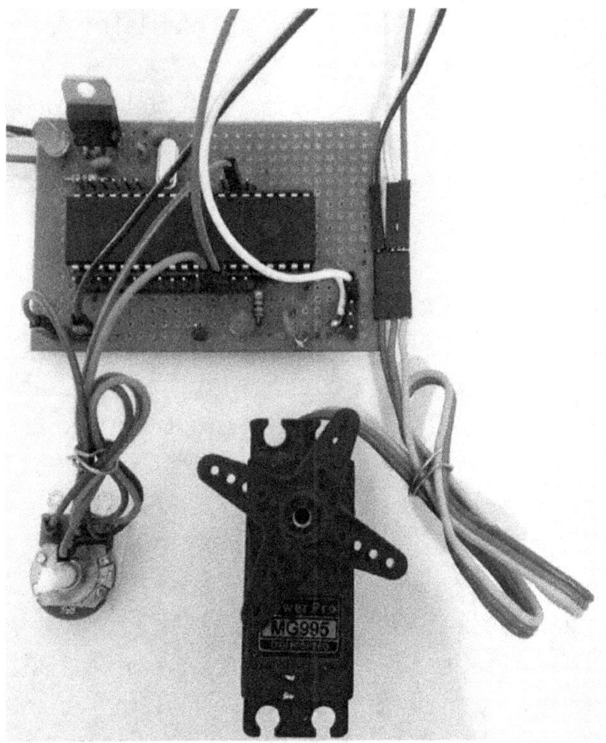

That is it!! We have interfaced a servo engine with a PIC Microcontroller, presently you can utilize your own innovativeness and discover applications for this. There are heaps of ventures out there which utilize a servo engine.

Code

```
#define _XTAL_FREQ 20000000

// CONFIG
#pragma config FOSC = HS      // Oscillator Selection
bits (HS oscillator)
#pragma config WDTE = OFF     // Watchdog Timer
Enable bit (WDT disabled)
#pragma config PWRTE = ON     // Power-up Timer
Enable bit (PWRT enabled)
#pragma config BOREN = ON     // Brown-out Reset
Enable bit (BOR enabled)
#pragma config LVP = OFF      // Low-Voltage (Single-Supply) In-Circuit Serial Programming Enable bit
(RB3 is digital I/O, HV on MCLR must be used for programming)
#pragma config CPD = OFF    // Data EEPROM Memory
Code Protection bit (Data EEPROM code protection off)
#pragma config WRT = OFF      // Flash Program Memory Write Enable bits (Write protection off; all program memory may be written to by EECON control)
#pragma config CP = OFF     // Flash Program Memory Code Protection bit (Code protection off)

// #pragma config statements should precede project
```

file includes.
// Use project enums instead of #define for ON and OFF.

#include <xc.h>

//TIMER0 8-bit $$RegValue = 256-((Delay * Fosc)/(Prescalar*4))$$

```c
char value = 0;
int on_time ;//= 150; //On-Time for the PWM signal
int count; //count gets incremented for every timer overlap
int pot_value;

/*********ADC Functions*********/
void ADC_Init()
{
 ADCON0 = 0x41; //ADC Module Turned ON and Clock is selected
 ADCON1 = 0xC0; //All pins as Analog Input
       //With reference voltages VDD and VSS
}
unsigned int ADC_Read(unsigned char channel)
{
 if(channel > 7) //If Invalid channel selected
  return 0;   //Return 0

 ADCON0 &= 0xC5; //Clearing the Channel Selection Bits
 ADCON0 |= channel<<3; //Setting the required Bits
  __delay_ms(2); //Acquisition time to charge hold capacitor
```

```c
GO_nDONE = 1; //Initializes A/D Conversion
  while(GO_nDONE); //Wait for A/D Conversion to
complete
 return ((ADRESH<<8)+ADRESL); //Returns Result
}
 //**************************************************//

void interrupt timer_isr()
{
  if(TMR0IF==1) // Timer has overflown
  {
      TMR0 = 252;    /*Load the timer Value, (Note:
Timervalue is 101 instaed of 100 as the
          TImer0 needs two instruction Cycles to start
incrementing TMR0 */
    TMR0IF=0;    // Clear timer interrupt flag
    count++;
  }


  if(count >= on_time)
  {
    RB0=1; // complement the value for blinking the
LEDs
  }


  if(count >= (on_time+(200-on_time)))
  {
   RB0=0;
   count=0;
  }
```

```c
}

void main()
{
/**************I/O PORT Initialization*************/
 TRISB = 0x00; //RB0 used as Servo signal pin
 TRISA = 0xFF; //Analog inputs
 //*********************************************** //

ADC_Init(); //Initializes ADC Module


    OPTION_REG = 0b00000100;  // Timer0 with ex-
ternal freq and 32 as prescaler
  TMR0=251;     // Load the time value for 1us delay-
Value can be between 0-256 only
  TMR0IE=1;     //Enable timer interrupt bit in PIE1
register
  GIE=1;      //Enable Global Interrupt
  PEIE=1;     //Enable the Peripheral Interrupt

  while(1)
  {
   pot_value = (ADC_Read(4))*0.039;
   on_time = (170-pot_value);
  }
}
```

◆ ◆ ◆

6. CREATING PWM UTILIZING PIC MICROCONTROLLER WITH MPLAB AND XC8

This is our tenth instructional exercise of Learning PIC microcontrollers utilizing MPLAB and XC8. Till now, we have secured numerous fundamental instructional exercises like LED flickering with PIC, Timers in PIC, interfacing LCD, interfacing 7-section, ADC utilizing PIC and so on. In the event that you are a flat out learner, at that point please visit the total rundown of PIC instructional exercises here and begin learning.

In this instructional exercise, we will figure out How to create PWM signals utilizing PIC PIC16F877A. Our PIC MCU has an uncommon module called Compare Capture module (CCP) which can be utilized to produce PWM signals. Here, we will produce a Pulse Width Modulation of 5 kHz with a variable obligation cycle from 0% to 100%. To fluctuate the obligation cycle we are utilizing a potentiometer, consequently it is prescribed to learn ADC instructional exercise before beginning with PWM. PWM module likewise utilizes clocks to set its recurrence subsequently figure out how to utilize clocks in advance here. Further, in this instructional exercise we will utilize a RC circuit and a LED to change over the PWM esteems to Analog voltage and use it for diminishing the LED light.

What is a PWM Signal?

Heartbeat Width Modulation (PWM) is a computerized signal which is most ordinarily utilized in charge hardware. This sign is set high (5v) along with low (0v) in a predefined time along with speed. The time during which the sign remains high is known as the "on schedule" and the time during which the sign remains low is known as the "off time". There are 2 significant parameters for a PWM as talked about underneath:

Obligation pattern of the PWM:

The level of time wherein the PWM signal stays HIGH (on schedule) is called as obligation cycle. In the event that the sign is consistently ON it is in 100% obligation cycle and on the off chance that it is constantly off it is 0% obligation cycle.

Obligation Cycle =Turn ON schedule/(Turn ON time

+ Turn OFF time)

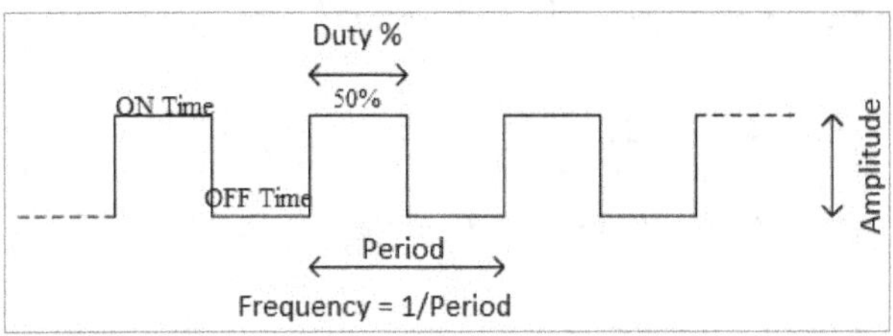

Recurrence of a PWM:

The recurrence of a PWM signal decides how quick a PWM finishes one period. One Period is finished ON and OFF of a PWM signal as appeared in the above figure. In our instructional exercise we will set a recurrence of 5KHz.

PWM utilizing PIC16F877A:

PWM signs can be created in our PIC Microcontroller by utilizing the CCP (Compare Capture PWM) module. The goals of our PWM signal is 10-piece, that is for an estimation of 0 there will be an obligation pattern of 0% and for an estimation of 1024 (2^10) there be an obligation pattern of 100%. There are 2 CCP modules in our PIC MCU (CCP1 And CCP2), this implies we can create two PWM flags on two distinct pins (pin 17 and 16) all the while, in our instructional exercise we are utilizing CCP1 to produce PWM flags on pin 17.

The accompanying registers are utilized to create PWM signals utilizing our PIC MCU:

- CCP1CON (CCP1 control Register)

- T2CON (Timer 2 Control Register)

- PR2 (Timer 2 modules Period Register)

- CCPR1L (CCP Register 1 Low)

Programming PIC to create Pulse Width Modulation signals:

In our program we will peruse an Analog voltage of 0-5v from a potentiometer along with guide it to 0-1024 utilizing our Analog to Digital Converter module. At that point we create a PWM signal with recurrence 5000Hz and differ its obligation cycle dependent on the information Analog voltage. That is 0-1024 will be changed over to 0%-100% Duty cycle. This instructional exercise accept that you have as of now figured out how to utilize ADC in PIC if not, read it from here, on the grounds that we will skip insights regarding it in this instructional exercise.

In this way, when the setup bits are set and program is composed to peruse an Analog worth, we can continue with PWM.

The accompanying advances ought to be taken while

designing the CCP module for PWM activity:

- Set the PWM time frame by keeping in touch with the PR2 register.

- Set the PWM obligation cycle by keeping in touch with the CCPR1L register and CCP1CON<5:4> bits.

- Make the CCP1 pin a yield by clearing the TRISC<2> bit.

- Set the TMR2 prescale esteem and empower Timer2 by writing to T2CON.

- Design the CCP1 module for Pulse Width Modulation activity.

There are 2 significant capacities in this program to produce PWM signals. One is the PWM_Initialize() work which will instate the registers required to set up PWM module and afterward set the recurrence at which the PWM ought to work, the other capacity is the PWM_Duty() work which will set the obligation pattern of the PWM signal in the necessary registers.

```
PWM_Initialize()

{

  PR2  =  (_XTAL_FREQ/(PWM_freq*4*TMR2PRE-
```

```
SCALE)) - 1; //Setting the PR2 formulae using Da-
tasheet // Makes the PWM work in 5KHZ


   CCP1M3 = 1; CCP1M2 = 1;  //Configure the CCP1
module


   T2CKPS0 = 1;T2CKPS1 = 0; TMR2ON = 1; //Con-
figure the Timer module


   TRISC2 = 0; // make port pin on C as output


}
```

The above capacity is the PWM introduce work, in this capacity The CCP1 module is set to utilize PWM by making the bit CCP1M3 and CCP1M2 as high.

CCP1CON REGISTER/CCP2CON REGISTER (ADDRESS 17h/1Dh)

U-0	U-0	R/W-0	R/W-0	R/W-0	R/W-0	R/W-0	R/W-0
—	—	CCPxX	CCPxY	CCPxM3	CCPxM2	CCPxM1	CCPxM0
bit 7							bit 0

bit 3-0   CCPxM3:CCPxM0: CCPx Mode Select bits

0000 = Capture/Compare/PWM disabled (resets CCPx module)
0100 = Capture mode, every **falling edge**
0101 = Capture mode, every **rising edge**
0110 = Capture mode, every **4th rising edge**
0111 = Capture mode, every **16th rising edge**
1000 = Compare mode, set **output on match** (CCPxIF bit is set)
1001 = Compare mode, clear **output on match** (CCPxIF bit is set)
1010 = Compare mode, generate **software interrupt on match** (CCPxIF bit is set, CCPx pin is unaffected)
1011 = Compare mode, trigger **special event** (CCPxIF bit is set, CCPx pin is unaffected), CCP1 resets TMR1; CCP2 **resets TMR1 and starts an A/D conversion** (if A/D module is enabled)
11xx = PWM mode

The clock module's prescaler is set by making the bit T2CKPS0 as high and T2CKPS1 as low the bit TMR2ON is set to begin the clock.

T2CON: TIMER2 CONTROL REGISTER (ADDRESS 12h)							
U-0	R/W-0	R/W-0	R/W-0	R/W-0	R/W-0	R/W-0	R/W-0
—	TOUTPS3	TOUTPS2	TOUTPS1	TOUTPS0	TMR2ON	T2CKPS1	T2CKPS0
bit 7							bit 0

bit 1-0   **T2CKPS1:T2CKPS0** Timer2 Clock Prescale Select bits
00 = Prescaler is 1
01 = Prescaler is 4
1x = Prescaler is 16

Presently, we require to set the Frequency of the PWM signal. The estimation of the recurrence must be kept in touch with the PR2 register. The ideal recurrence can be set by utilizing the beneath formulae

PWM Period = [(PR2) + 1] * 4 * TOSC * (TMR2 Prescale Value)

Revamping these formulae to get PR2 will give

PR2 = (Period / (4 * Tosc * TMR2 Prescale)) - 1

We realize that Period = (1/PWM_freq) and Tosc = (1/_XTAL_FREQ). Therefore.....

```
PR2 = (_XTAL_FREQ/ (PWM_freq*4*TMR2PRE-
SCALE))-1;
```

When the recurrence is set this capacity need not be called again except if and until we have to change the recurrence once more. In our instructional exercise I have doled out PWM_freq = 5000; with the goal that we can get a 5 KHz working recurrence for our PWM signal.

Presently let us set the obligation pattern of the PWM by utilizing the underneath work

```
PWM_Duty(unsigned int duty)

{

  if(duty<1023)

  {

    duty = ((float)duty/1023)*(_XTAL_FREQ/(PW-
M_freq*TMR2PRESCALE)); // On reducing //duty
= (((float)duty/1023)*(1/PWM_freq)) / ((1/_XTAL_
FREQ)*TMR2PRESCALE);

  CCP1X = duty & 1; //Store the 1st bit
```

```
    CCP1Y = duty & 2; //Store the 0th bit

    CCPR1L = duty>>2;// Store the remining 8 bit


  }


}
```

Our PWM signal has 10-piece goals consequently this worth can't be put away in a solitary register since our PIC has just 8-piece information lines. So we have use to other two bits of CCP1CON<5:4> (CCP1X and CCP1Y) to store the last two LSB and afterward store the staying 8 bits in the CCPR1L Register.

The PWM obligation process duration can be determined by utilizing the underneath formulae:

PWM Duty Cycle = (CCPRIL:CCP1CON<5:4>) * Tosc * (TMR2 Prescale Value)

Modifying these formulae to get estimation of CCPR1L and CCP1CON will give:

CCPRIL:CCP1Con<5:4> = PWM Duty Cycle / (Tosc * TMR2 Prescale Value)

The estimation of our ADC will be 0-1024 we need that to be in 0%-100% subsequently, PWM Duty Cycle = obligation/1023. Further to change over this obligation cycle into a timeframe we need to duplicate it with the period (1/PWM_freq)

We additionally realize that Tosc = (1/PWM_freq), subsequently..

```
Duty = ( ( (float)duty/1023) * (1/PWM_freq) ) / ( (1/_XTAL_FREQ) * TMR2PRESCALE);
```

Settling the above condition will give us:

```
Duty = ( (float)duty/1023) * (_XTAL_FREQ / (PWM_freq*TMR2PRESCALE));
```

Schematics and Testing:

As common let us check the yield utilizing Proteus reenactment. The Circuit Diagram is demonstrated as follows.

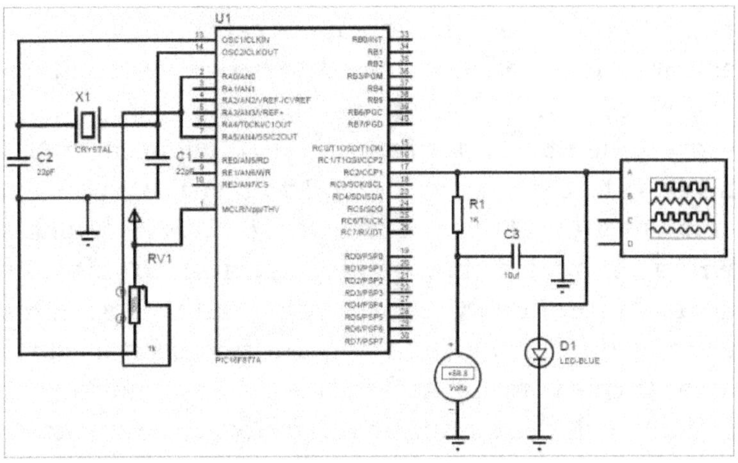

Interface a potentiometer to seventh pin to manage in a voltage of 0-5. CCP1 module is with pin 17 (RC2), here the PWM will be created which can be checked utilizing the Digital oscilloscope. Further to change over this into a variable voltage we have utilized a RC-channel and a LED to check the yield without a degree.

What is a RC-Filter?

A RC channel or a Low pass channel is a straightforward circuit with two inactive components to be specific the resistor and the capacitor. These two segments are used to channel the recurrence of our PWM sign and make it a variable DC voltage.

On the off chance that we inspect the circuit, when a variable voltage is applied to the contribution of R, the capacitor C will start to charge. Presently dependent on the estimation of the capacitor, the capacitor will set aside some effort to get completely energized, when charged it will hinder the DC current (Remember capacitors square DC yet permits AC) henceforth the information DC voltage will show up over the yield. The high recurrence PWM (AC signal) will be grounded through the capacitor. In this way an unadulterated DC is gotten over the capacitor. An estimation of 1000Ohm and 1uf was seen as suitable for this venture. Ascertaining the estimations of R and C includes circuit investigation utilizing move work, which is out of extent of this instructional exercise.

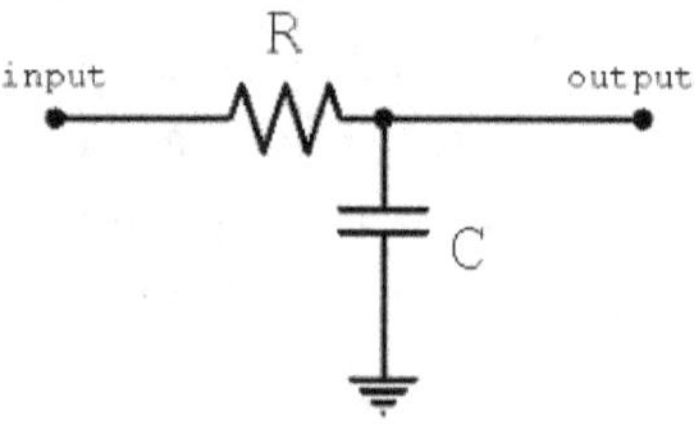

The yield of the program can be confirmed utilizing the Digital Oscilloscope as demonstrated as follows, fluctuate the Potentiometer and the Duty pattern of the PWM should change. We can likewise see the yield voltage of the RC circuit utilizing the Voltmeter. In case everything is filling in true to form we can proceed with our equipment.

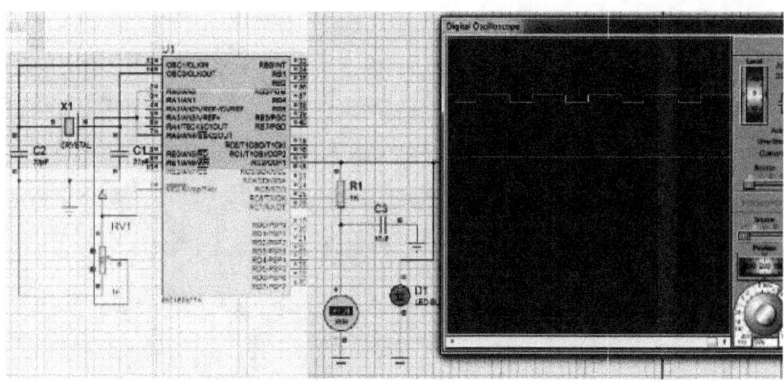

Taking a shot at Hardware:

The equipment arrangement of the venture is extremely basic, we are simply going to reuse our PIC Perfboard demonstrated as follows.

We will likewise require a potentiometer to take care of in the simple voltage, I have joined some female end wires to my pot (demonstrated as follows) so we can straightforwardly interface them to the PIC Perf board.

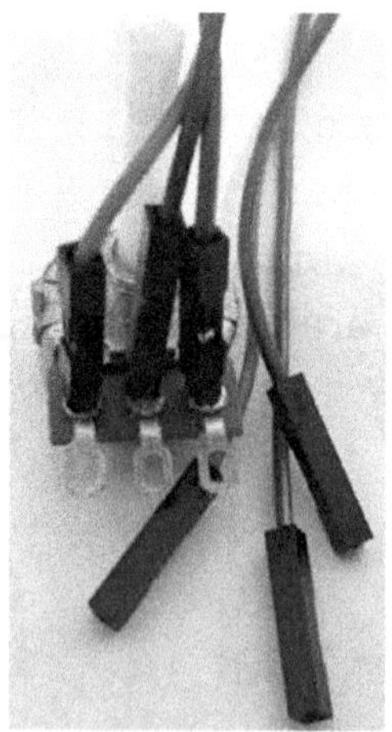

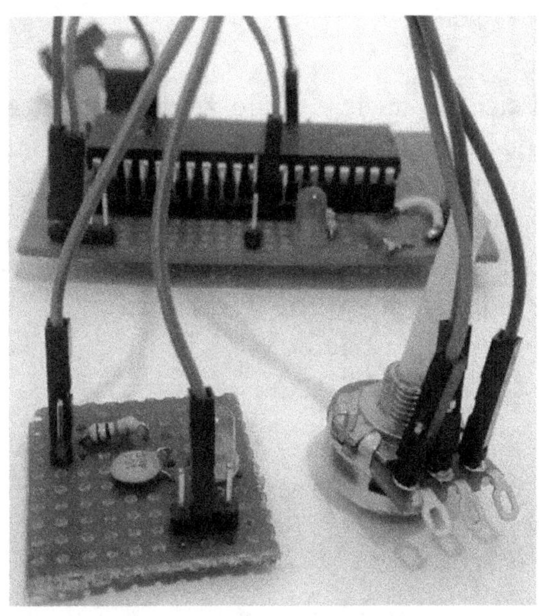

At long last to check the yield we need a RC circuit and a LED to perceive how the PWM signal functions, I have basically utilized a little perf board and bound the RC circuit and the LED (to control splendor) on to it as demonstrated as follows

We can utilize basic female to female interfacing wires and associate them as per the schematics appeared previously. When the association is done, transfer the program to the PIC utilizing our pickit3 and you ought to have the option to get a variable voltage dependent on the contribution of your potentiometer. The variable yield is utilized to control the splendor of the LED here.

I utilized my multimeter to quantify the variable yields, we can likewise see the splendor of the LED getting changed for various voltage levels.

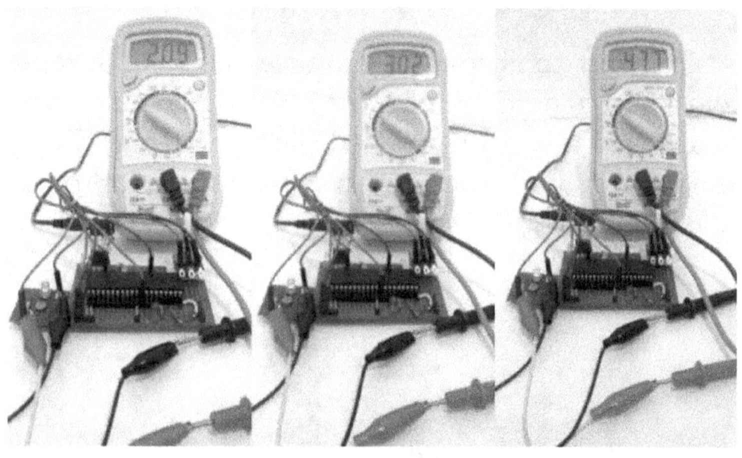

That is it we have customized to peruse the Analog voltage from the POT and convert into PWM signals which thus have been changed over into Variable voltage utilizing RC channel and the outcome is confirmed utilizing our equipment. In case you have some uncertainty or stall out some place compassionately utilize the remark segment beneath, we will be glad to get you out.

Additionally check our other PWM Tutorials on different microcontrollers:

- Raspberry Pi PWM Tutorial

- PWM with Arduino Due

- Arduino Based LED Dimmer utilizing PWM

- Force LED Dimmer utilizing ATmega32 Microcontroller

Code

```
// CONFIG
#pragma config FOSC = HS        // Oscillator Selection bits (HS oscillator)
#pragma config WDTE = OFF       // Watchdog Timer Enable bit (WDT disabled)
#pragma config PWRTE = ON       // Power-up Timer Enable bit (PWRT enabled)
#pragma config BOREN = OFF      // Brown-out Reset Enable bit (BOR disabled)
#pragma config LVP = ON         // Low-Voltage (Single-Supply) In-Circuit Serial Programming Enable bit (RB3/PGM pin has PGM function; low-voltage pro-
```

```c
gramming enabled)
#pragma config CPD = OFF    // Data EEPROM Memory
Code Protection bit (Data EEPROM code protection
off)
#pragma config WRT = OFF     // Flash Program Mem-
ory Write Enable bits (Write protection off; all pro-
gram memory may be written to by EECON control)
#pragma config CP = OFF     // Flash Program Memory
Code Protection bit (Code protection off)

#define _XTAL_FREQ 20000000
#define TMR2PRESCALE 4

#include <xc.h>

long PWM_freq = 5000;

PWM_Initialize()
{
    PR2    =    (_XTAL_FREQ/(PWM_freq*4*TMR2PRE-
SCALE)) - 1; //Setting the PR2 formulae using Da-
tasheet // Makes the PWM work in 5KHZ
  CCP1M3 = 1; CCP1M2 = 1; //Configure the CCP1 mod-
ule
  T2CKPS0 = 1;T2CKPS1 = 0; TMR2ON = 1; //Configure
the Timer module
  TRISC2 = 0; // make port pin on C as output
}

PWM_Duty(unsigned int duty)
{
  if(duty<1023)
 {
```

```c
    duty = ((float)duty/1023)*(_XTAL_FREQ/(PWM_freq*TMR2PRESCALE)); // On reducing //duty = ((((float)duty/1023)*(1/PWM_freq)) / ((1/_XTAL_FREQ)*TMR2PRESCALE);
  CCP1X = duty & 1; //Store the 1st bit
  CCP1Y = duty & 2; //Store the 0th bit
  CCPR1L = duty>>2;// Store the remining 8 bit
  }
}

void ADC_Initialize()
{
 ADCON0 = 0b01000001; //ADC ON and Fosc/16 is selected
 ADCON1 = 0b11000000; // Internal reference voltage is selected
}
unsigned int ADC_Read(unsigned char channel)
{
 ADCON0 &= 0x11000101; //Clearing the Channel Selection Bits
 ADCON0 |= channel<<3; //Setting the required Bits
 __delay_ms(2); //Acquisition time to charge hold capacitor
 GO_nDONE = 1; //Initializes A/D Conversion
  while(GO_nDONE); //Wait for A/D Conversion to complete
 return ((ADRESH<<8)+ADRESL); //Returns Result
}
void main()
{
```

```c
 int adc_value;
TRISC = 0x00; //PORTC as output
TRISA = 0xFF; //PORTA as input
TRISD = 0x00;
ADC_Initialize(); //Initializes ADC Module
PWM_Initialize();  //This sets the PWM frequency of
PWM1

do
{
  adc_value = ADC_Read(4); //Reading Analog Chan-
nel 0
 PWM_Duty(adc_value);


   __delay_ms(50);


}while(1); //Infinite Loop


}
```

❖ ❖ ❖

7. UTILIZING ADC MODULE OF PIC MICROCONTROLLER WITH MPLAB AND XC8

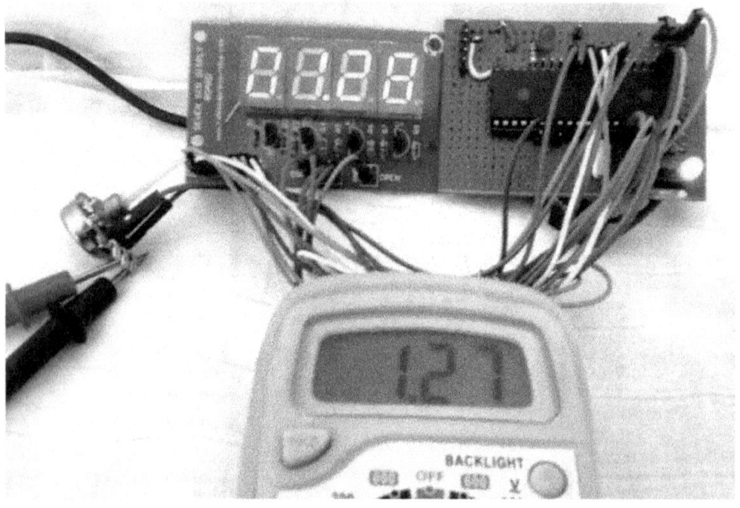

This is our ninth instructional exercise of Learning PIC microcontrollers utilizing MPLAB and XC8. Till now, we have secured numerous essential instructional exercise like beginning with MPLABX, LED flickering with PIC, Timers in PIC, interfacing LCD, interfacing 7-portion and so on. In the event that you are an outright tenderfoot, at that point please visit the total rundown of PIC instructional exercises here and begin learning.

In this instructional exercise, we will figure out How

to Use ADC with our PIC microcontroller PICF877A. The majority of the Microcontroller undertakings will include an (Analog to Digital converter) in it, since it is one the most utilized approaches to peruse information from this present reality. Practically all the sensors like temperature sensor, motion sensor, pressure sensor, current sensors, voltage sensors, spinners, accelerometers, separation sensor, and pretty much every known sensor or transducer creates a simple voltage of 0V to 5V dependent on the sensors perusing. A temperature sensor for example may give out 2.1V when the temperature is 25C along with go upto 4.7 when the temperature is 60C. So as to know the temperature of this present reality, the MCU needs to simply peruse the yield voltage of this temperature sensor and relate it to this present reality temperature. Henceforth ADC is a significant work apparatus for MCU activities and lets figure out how we can utilize it on our PIC16F877A.

Likewise check our past articles on utilizing ADC in different microcontrollers:

- How to Use ADC in Arduino Uno?

- Raspberry Pi ADC Tutorial

- Interfacing ADC0808 with 8051 Microcontroller

ADC in PIC Microcontroller PIC16F877A:

There are numerous kinds of ADC accessible and every one has its own speed and goals. The elaborately recognized sorts of ADCs are streak, progressive estimate, and sigma-delta. The kind of ADC utilized in PIC16F877A is called as the Successive estimation ADC or SAR in short. So how about we become well known with somewhat about SAR ADC before we initiate utilizing it.

Progressive Approximation ADC: The SAR ADC works with the assistance of a comparator and some rationale discussions. This kind of ADC utilizes a reference voltage (which is variable) and contrasts the information voltage along with the reference voltage utilizing a comparator and distinction, which will be a computerized yield, is spared from the Most noteworthy piece (MSB). The speed of the examination relies upon the Clock recurrence (Fosc) on which the PIC is working.

Since we know a few essentials on ADC, lets open our datasheet and figure out how to utilize the ADC on our PIC16F877A MCU. The PIC we are utilizing has 10-piece 8-channel ADC. This implies the yield estimation of our ADC will be 0-1024 (2^10) along with there are 8 pins (channels) on our MCU which can peruse simple voltage. The worth 1024 is acquired by 2^10 since our ADC is 10 piece. The eight pins which can peruse the simple voltage are referenced in the datasheet. Lets take a gander at the image beneath.

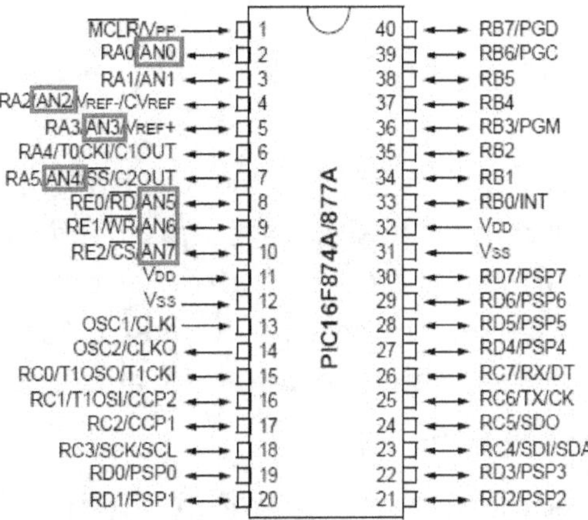

The simple channels AN0 to AN7 are featured for you. Just these pins will have the option to peruse simple voltage. So before perusing an information voltage we require to indicate in our code which channel must be utilized to peruse the information voltage. In this instructional exercise we will utilize channel 4 with a potentiometer to peruse the simple voltage at this channel.

The A/D module has four registers which must be arranged to peruse information from the Input pins. These registers are:

• A/D Result High Register (ADRESH)

• A/D Result Low Register (ADRESL)

• A/D Control Register 0 (ADCON0)

• A/D Control Register 1 (ADCON1)

Programming for ADC:

The program for utilizing ADC with PIC Microcontroller is extremely basic, we simply need to comprehend these four registers and afterward perusing any simple voltage will be straightforward. As normal instate the arrangement bits and how about we initiate with the void primary().

Inside the void primary() we require to introduce our ADC by utilizing the ADCON1 register and ADCON0 register. The ADCON0 register has the accompanying bits:

ADCON0 REGISTER (ADDRESS 1Fh)							
R/W-0	R/W-0	R/W-0	R/W-0	R/W-0	R/W-0	U-0	R/W-0
ADCS1	ADCS0	CHS2	CHS1	CHS0	GO/$\overline{\text{DONE}}$	—	ADON
bit 7							bit 0

In this register we require to turn on the ADC module by doing ADON=1 along with turn on the A/D Conversion Clock by utilizing the bits ADCS1 and ADCS0 bits, the rest won't be set until further notice. In our program the A/D transformation clock is chosen as Fosc/16 you can attempt your own frequencies and perceive how the outcome changes. Complete subtleties accessible on datasheet's page 127. Henceforth ADCON0 will be initialised as follows.

```
ADCON0 = 0b01000001;
```

Presently the ADCON1 register has the accompanying bits:

ADCON1 REGISTER (ADDRESS 9Fh)							
R/W-0	R/W-0	U-0	U-0	R/W-0	R/W-0	R/W-0	R/W-0
ADFM	ADCS2	—	—	PCFG3	PCFG2	PCFG1	PCFG0
bit 7							bit 0

In this register we need to make A/D Result Format Select piece high by ADFM=1 and make ADCS2 =1 to choose the Fosc/16 once more. Different bits stay zero as we have intended to utilize the inward reference voltage. Complete subtleties accessible on datasheet page 128. Thus ADCON1 will we set as follows.

```
ADCON1 = 0x11000000;
```

Presently in the wake of introducing the ADC module inside our primary capacity, lets get into the while circle and begin perusing the ADC esteems. To peruse an ADC esteem the accompanying advances must be followed.

- Introduce the ADC Module

- Select the simple channel

- Start ADC by making Go/Done piece high

- Hang tight for the Go/DONE piece to get low

- Get the ADC result from ADRESH and ADRESL register

1. Instate the ADC Module: We have as of now figured out how to introduce an ADC so we simply call this beneath capacity to instate the ADC

The void ADC_Initialize() work is be as per the following.

```
void ADC_Initialize()

{

  ADCON0 = 0b01000001; //ADC ON and Fosc/16 is selected

  ADCON1 = 0b11000000; // Internal reference voltage is selected

}
```

2. Select the simple channel: Now we require to choose which channel we are going to use to peruse the ADC esteem. Lets make a capacity for this, with the goal that it will be simple for us to move between each channel inside the while circle.

```
unsigned int ADC_Read(unsigned char channel)

{

    //****Selecting the channel**///

  ADCON0 &= 0x11000101; //Clearing the Channel
Selection Bits

  ADCON0 |= channel<<3; //Setting the required
Bits

  //**Channel selection complete***///

}
```

At that point channel to be chosen is gotten inside the variable channel. In the line

```
ADCON0 &= 0x1100101;
```

The past channel determination (assuming any) is cleared. This is finished by utilizing the bitwise and administrator "and". The bits 3, 4 and 5 are compelled to be 0 while the others are left to be in their past qualities.

At that point the ideal channel is chosen by left moving the channel number thrice and setting the bits utilizing the bitwise or administrator "|".

```
ADCON0 |= channel<<3; //Setting the required Bits
```

3. Start ADC by making Go/Done piece high: Once the channel is chosen we require to begin the ADC transformation just by making the GO_nDONE bit high:

```
GO_nDONE = 1; //Initializes A/D Conversion
```

4. Sit tight for the Go/DONE piece to get low: The GO/DONE piece will remain high until the ADC change has been finished, henceforth we require to hold up till this bit goes low once more. This should be possible by utilizing some time circle.

```
while(GO_nDONE); //Wait for A/D Conversion to
complete
```

Note: Placing a semi-colon close to while will do the program to be held there till the condtion of the while circle is bogus.

5. Get the Analog to Digital Converter result from ADRESH along with ADRESL register: When the Go/DONE piece gets low again it implies that the ADC transformation is finished. The aftereffect of the ADC will be a 10-piece esteem. Since our MCU is a 8-piece MCU the outcome is part into upper 8-piece and the lower 2-bits. The upper 8-piece result is put away in the register ADRESH and the lower 2-piece is put away in the register ADRESL. Subsequently we require to include these to registers to get our 10-piece ADC esteem. This outcome is returned by the capacity as demonstrated as follows:

```
return ((ADRESH<<8)+ADRESL); //Returns Result
```

The total capacity which is utilized to choose the ADC channel, trigger the ADC and return the outcome is appeared here.

```
unsigned int ADC_Read(unsigned char channel)

{

  ADCON0 &= 0x11000101; //Clearing the Channel Selection Bits

  ADCON0 |= channel<<3; //Setting the required Bits
```

```c
    __delay_ms(2); //Acquisition time to charge hold
  capacitor

  GO_nDONE = 1; //Initializes A/D Conversion

  while(GO_nDONE); //Wait for A/D Conversion to
  complete

  return ((ADRESH<<8)+ADRESL); //Returns Result

}
```

Presently we have a capacity which will accept the channel choice as information and return us the ADC esteem. Henceforth we can legitimately call this capacity inside our while circle, since we are perusing the simple voltage from direct 4 in this instructional exercise, the capacity call will be as per the following.

```c
i = (ADC_Read(4)); //store the result of adc in "i".
```

So as to imagine the yield of our ADC we will require a type of show modules like the LCD or the 7-section. In this instructional exercise we are utilizing a 7-portion show to confirm the yield. In case you require to realize how to utilize 7-portion with pic follow the instructional exercise here.

The total code is given beneath toward the end.

Equipment Setup and Testing:

As normal mimic the code utilizing Proteus before really go with our equipment, the schematics of the undertaking is demonstrated as follows:

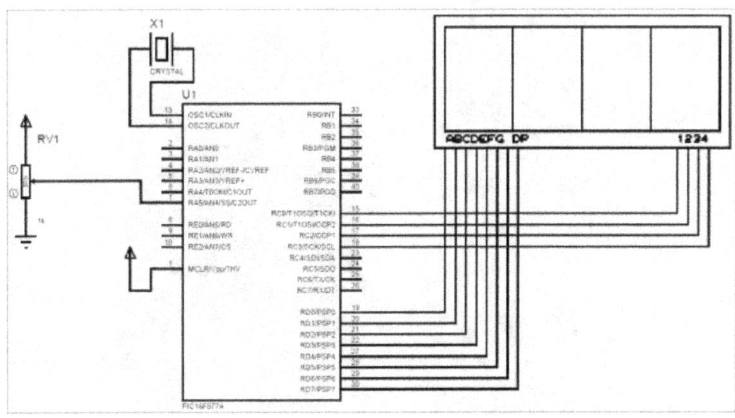

Associations of 4-digit seven section show module with PIC microcontroller are same as the past venture, we have quite recently added a potentiometer to the pin 7 which is the simple channel 4. By fluctuating the pot, a variable voltage will be sent to the MCU which will be perused by the ADC module and showed on the 7-fragment show Module. Check the past instructional exercise to become well known with 4-digit 7-portion show and its interfacing with PIC MCU.

Here we have utilized a similar PIC Microcontroller board which we have made in LED flickering Tutorial. In the wake of guaranteeing association transfer the program into PIC and you should see a yield this way

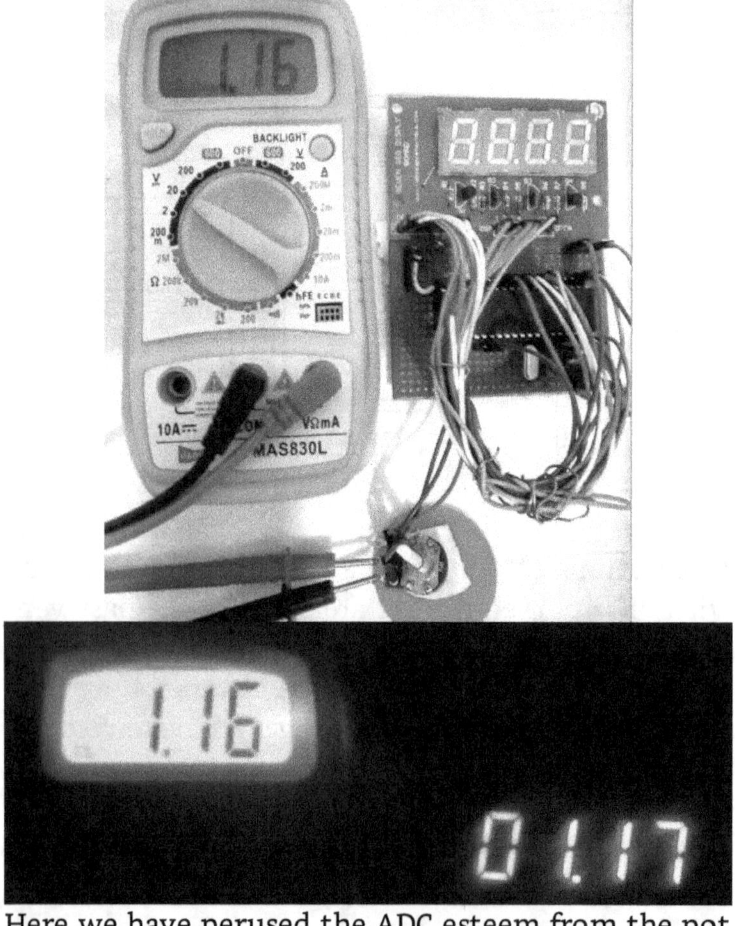

Here we have perused the ADC esteem from the pot and changed over it to the real voltage by mapping

the 0-1024 yield as 0-5 volts (as appeared in program). The worth is then shown on the 7-portion and confirmed utilizing the multimeter.

That is it, presently we are prepared to utilize all the Analog Sensors accessible in the market, feel free to attempt this and on the off chance that you have any issues as normal utilize the remark area, we will be glad to get you out.

Code

```
// CONFIG
#pragma config FOSC = HS      // Oscillator Selection bits (HS oscillator)
#pragma config WDTE = OFF     // Watchdog Timer Enable bit (WDT disabled)
#pragma config PWRTE = ON     // Power-up Timer Enable bit (PWRT enabled)
#pragma config BOREN = ON     // Brown-out Reset Enable bit (BOR enabled)
#pragma config LVP = OFF      // Low-Voltage (Single-Supply) In-Circuit Serial Programming Enable bit (RB3 is digital I/O, HV on MCLR must be used for programming)
#pragma config CPD = OFF    // Data EEPROM Memory Code Protection bit (Data EEPROM code protection off)
#pragma config WRT = OFF    // Flash Program Memory Write Enable bits (Write protection off; all program memory may be written to by EECON control)
```

```c
#pragma config CP = OFF     // Flash Program Memory
Code Protection bit (Code protection off)

// #pragma config statements should precede project
file includes.
// Use project enums instead of #define for ON and
OFF.

#include <xc.h>
#define _XTAL_FREQ 20000000

//***Define the signal pins of all four displays***//
#define s1 RC0
#define s2 RC1
#define s3 RC2
#define s4 RC3
//***End of definition**////

void ADC_Initialize()
{
 ADCON0 = 0b01000001; //ADC ON and Fosc/16 is selected
  ADCON1 = 0b11000000; // Internal reference voltage is selected
}

unsigned int ADC_Read(unsigned char channel)
{
 ADCON0 &= 0x11000101; //Clearing the Channel Selection Bits
 ADCON0 |= channel<<3; //Setting the required Bits
  __delay_ms(2); //Acquisition time to charge hold capacitor
```

```c
 GO_nDONE = 1; //Initializes A/D Conversion
  while(GO_nDONE); //Wait for A/D Conversion to
complete
 return ((ADRESH<<8)+ADRESL); //Returns Result
}

void main()
{ int a,b,c,d,e,f,g,h,adc; //just variables
int i = 0; //the 4-digit value that is to be displayed
int flag =0; //for creating delay

unsigned int seg[]={0X3F, //Hex value to display the
number 0
        0X06, //Hex value to display the number 1
        0X5B, //Hex value to display the number 2
        0X4F, //Hex value to display the number 3
        0X66, //Hex value to display the number 4
        0X6D, //Hex value to display the number 5
        0X7C, //Hex value to display the number 6
        0X07, //Hex value to display the number 7
        0X7F, //Hex value to display the number 8
        0X6F //Hex value to display the number 9
        }; //End of Array for displaying numbers from
0 to 9

//*****I/O Configuration****//
TRISC=0X00;
PORTC=0X00;
TRISD=0x00;
PORTD=0X00;
//***End of I/O configuration**///

ADC_Initialize();
```

```c
#define _XTAL_FREQ 20000000
while(1)
{


    if(flag>=50) //wait till flag reaches 100
{
  adc = (ADC_Read(4));
  i = adc*0.488281;
    flag=0; //only if flag is hundred "i" will get the ADC
value
}
flag++; //increment flag for each flash

 //***Splitting "i" into four digits***//
a=i%10;//4th digit is saved here
b=i/10;
c=b%10;//3rd digit is saved here
d=b/10;
e=d%10; //2nd digit is saved here
f=d/10;
g=f%10; //1st digit is saved here
h=f/10;
//***End of splitting***//

PORTD=seg[g];s1=1; //Turn ON display 1 and print
4th digit
__delay_ms(5);s1=0;   //Turn OFF display 1 after 5ms
delay
PORTD=seg[e];RD7=1;s2=1; //Turn ON display 2 and
print 3rd digit
__delay_ms(5);s2=0;   //Turn OFF display 2 after 5ms
```

```
delay
PORTD=seg[c];s3=1; //Turn ON  display 3 and print
2nd digit
__delay_ms(5);s3=0;   //Turn OFF display 3 after 5ms
delay
PORTD=seg[a];s4=1; //Turn ON display 4 and print 1st
digit
__delay_ms(5);s4=0;   //Turn OFF display 4 after 5ms
delay


}
}
```

◆ ◆ ◆

8. 7 SEGMENT DISPLAY INTERFACING WITH PIC MICROCONTROLLER

This is our eighth instructional exercise of Learning PIC microcontrollers utilizing MPLAB and XC8. We have come up right from introducing MPLABX to utilizing a Liquid Crystal Display with PIC MCU. In case you are new here, at that point take a gander at past instructional exercises where you can learn clocks, flickering LED, interfacing LCD along with etc.. You can discover all our PIC Tutorials here. In our last instructional exercise we perceived how we can create Custom characters with our 16*2 LCD show, presently let us furnish our self with another sort of show module called the 7-portion show and interface it with PIC Microcontroller.

Albeit 16x2 LCD is substantially more agreeable than 7-section show yet there are scarcely any situations where a 7-fragment show would come in handier than a LCD show. LCD experiences the downside of having low character size and will be pointless excess for your undertaking in case you are simply intending to show some numeric qualities. 7-portions likewise have the preferred position against poor lighting condition and can be seen from ale edges than an ordinary LCD screen. In this way, let us begin knowing it.

7-Segment and 4-Digit 7-Segment Display Module:

7 Segment Display has seven sections in it and each portion has one LED inside it to show the numbers by illuminating the comparing fragments. Like in the event that you need the 7-portion to show the number "5" at that point you have to sparkle fragment a,f,g,c, and d by making their comparing pins high. There are 2 sorts of 7-section shows: Common Cathode and Common Anode, here we are utilizing Common Cathode seven fragment show. Study 7 portion show here.

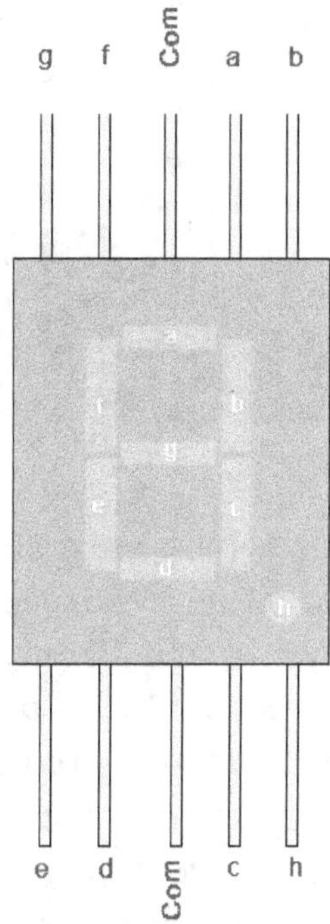

Presently we realize how to show our ideal numeric character on a solitary 7-fragment show. Yet, it is entirely apparent that we would require more than one 7-portion show to pass on any data that is more than 1 digit. In this lines, in this instructional exercise we will use a 4-digit 7-Segment Display Module as demonstrated as follows.

As should be obvious there are 4 Seven Segment Displays associated together. We realize that every 7-fragment module will have 10 pins and for 4 seven section shows there would be 40 pins altogether and it would be rushed for anybody to bind them on a dab board, so I would energetically prescribe anybody to purchase a module or make your own PCB for utilizing a 4-digit 7-portion show. The association schematic for the equivalent is demonstrated as follows:

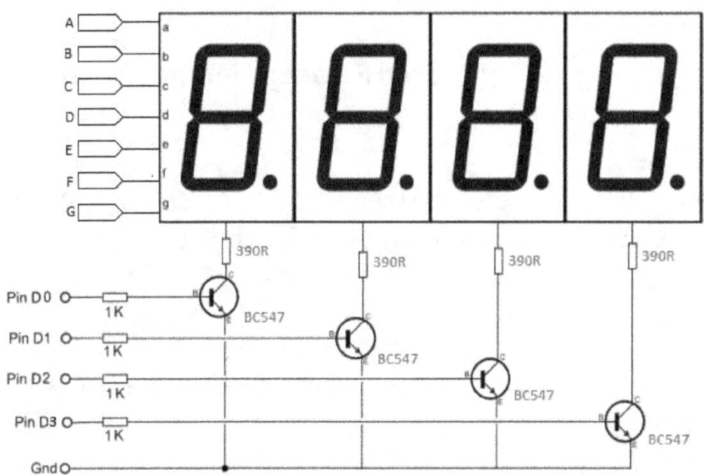

To see how 4-digit seven section module functions we need to investigate the above schematics, as indicated the A pins of each of the 4 presentation is associated with accumulate as one An and the equivalent for B,C.... upto DP. All in all, fundamentally in case trigger An on, at that point every one of the four An's ought to go high right?

In any case, that doesn't occur. We have extra four pins from D0 to D3 (D0, D1, D2 and D3) which can be utilized to control which show out of the four ought to go high. For instance: If I need my yield to be available just on the second showcase then just D1 ought to be made high while keeping different pins (D0, D2, and D3) as low. Basically we can choose which show needs to go dynamic utilizing the pins from D0 to D3 and what character to be show utilizing the pins from A to DP.

Interfacing 4-Digit Seven Segment Module with PIC Microcontroller:

Here we have utilized PIC microcontroller PIC16F877A and the schematic for the circuit is demonstrated as follows.

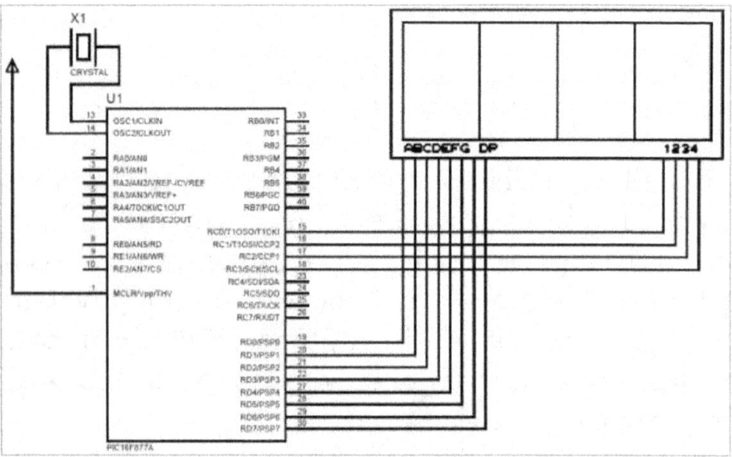

We have 12 yield pins from the module out of which 8 is utilized to show the characters and four is utilized to choose one presentation out of four. Thus all the 8 character pins are allocated to PORTD and the showcase choice pins are appointed to initial four pins of PORTC.

Note: Ground pin of the module ought to likewise be associated with the ground of the MCU which isn't appeared here.

Programming utilizing PIC16F877A:

Presently, that we know how this module really functions, let us find how to program PIC16F877A to make it show a 4 digit number. Let us increase a variable from 0 to 1000 along with print it on the 7-fragment show. Dispatch the MPLABX program and make new task, let us start with the setup bits.

```
#pragma config FOSC = HS     // Oscillator Selection
bits (HS oscillator)

#pragma config WDTE = OFF     // Watchdog Timer
Enable bit (WDT disabled)

#pragma config PWRTE = ON     // Power-up Timer
Enable bit (PWRT enabled)

#pragma config BOREN = ON     // Brown-out Reset
Enable bit (BOR enabled)

#pragma config LVP = OFF    // Low-Voltage (Single-
Supply) In-Circuit Serial Programming Enable bit
(RB3 is digital I/O, HV on MCLR must be used for
programming)

#pragma config CPD = OFF     // Data EEPROM Mem-
ory Code Protection bit (Data EEPROM code pro-
```

tection off)

#pragma config WRT = OFF   // Flash Program Memory Write Enable bits (Write protection off; all program memory may be written to by EECON control)

#pragma config CP = OFF   // Flash Program Memory Code Protection bit (Code protection off)

As normal we utilize the set design bits window to set these bits. On the off chance that you don't know what they mean, at that point visit the LED squinting instructional exercise here.

Next let us characterize the yield pins for flipping between every digit of the presentation.

```
//***Define the signal pins of all four displays***//

#define s1 RC0

#define s2 RC1

#define s3 RC2

#define s4 RC3

//***End of definition**////
```

Here the pins RC0, RC1, RC2 and RC3 are utilized for choosing between the four digits of our 7-section show module. These pins are characterized as s1, s2, s3 along with s4 individually.

Next let us bounce into void primary(), inside which we have the accompanying variable assertion:

int i = 0; //the 4-digit value that is to be displayed

int flag =0; //for creating delay

unsigned int a,b,c,d,e,f,g,h; //just variables

unsigned int seg[]={0X3F, //Hex value to display the number 0

0X06, //Hex value to display the number 1

0X5B, //Hex value to display the number 2

0X4F, //Hex value to display the number 3

0X66, //Hex value to display the number 4

0X6D, //Hex value to display the num-

```
ber 5

            0X7C, //Hex value to display the num-
ber 6


            0X07, //Hex value to display the num-
ber 7


            0X7F, //Hex value to display the num-
ber 8


            0X6F  //Hex value to display the num-
ber 9


            }; //End of Array for displaying numbers
from 0 to 9
```

Here the factors I and banner are utilized for putting away the qualities to be shown and making a postponement separately. The unsigned whole number factors a to h are utilized to break the four digit numbers into single digits and store them (which will be clarified later here).

One key thing to note here is the "seg[]" cluster presentation. In this program we are utilizing another information type called Array. Cluster is only an assortment of comparable information type esteems. Here, we have utilized this exhibit to store all the comparable hex qualities for showing a number from 0 to 9.

The location of the cluster consistently begins from zero. So this cluster will have the hex estimation of a numeric number (0-9) put away in the location which is same as that of the number as demonstrated as follows

Variable:	seg[0]	seg[1]	seg[2]	seg[3]	seg[4]	seg[5]	seg[6]	seg[7]	seg[8]	seg[9]
Hex Code:	OX3F	OX06	OX5B	OX4F	OX66	OX6D	OX7C	OX07	OX7F	OX6F
Eq. Numeric number:	0	1	2	3	4	5	6	7	8	9

So essentially, in case you require to show the number 0 on your 7-fragment you can call seg[0], in like manner in case you require to show the number 6 you simply require to utilize seg[6].

To see how the HEX worth was really gotten let us investigate the beneath table. The equal HEX an incentive for every decimal number is put away in the exhibit with the goal that it very well may be called to show one specific number.

Number	gfedcba	Hexadecimal
0	0111111	3F
1	0000110	06
2	1011011	5B
3	1001111	4F
4	1100110	66
5	1101101	6D
6	1111101	7D
7	0000111	07
8	1111111	7F
9	1101111	6F

Presently, let us proceed onward to the following piece of the code which is the I/O setup:

```
//*****I/O Configuration****//

TRISC=0X00;

PORTC=0X00;

TRISD=0x00;

PORTD=0X00;

//***End of I/O configuration**///
```

I/O arrangement is straightforward on the grounds that all the pins on our 7-fragment are yield pins, and the associations are appeared in the circuit chart above, so just proclaim them as yields and introduce them to zero.

Presently let us bounce into our interminable circle (while(1)). Here we require to part the estimation of "I" into four digits and show them on the 7-portion. First let us initiate by parting the incentive on "I"

```
//***Splitting "i" into four digits***//
```

```
a=i%10;//4th digit is saved here

b=i/10;

c=b%10;//3rd digit is saved here

d=b/10;

e=d%10; //2nd digit is saved here

f=d/10;

g=f%10; //1st digit is saved here

h=f/10;

//***End of splitting***//
```

By utilizing basic modulus and division activity the 4 digit number (I) is isolated into singular numbers. For our situation let us take a model where the estimation of "I" is 4578. At that point toward the finish of this procedure the variable g=4, e=5, c=7, and a=8. So now it will be anything but difficult to show every digit by essentially utilizing that variable.

```
PORTD=seg[g];s1=1; //Turn ON display 1 and print
4th digit

__delay_ms(5);s1=0;    //Turn OFF display 1 after
```

```
5ms delay

PORTD=seg[e];s2=1; //Turn ON display 2 and print
3rd digit


__delay_ms(5);s2=0;    //Turn OFF display 2 after
5ms delay


PORTD=seg[c];s3=1; //Turn ON display 3 and print
2nd digit


__delay_ms(5);s3=0;    //Turn OFF display 3 after
5ms delay


PORTD=seg[a];s4=1; //Turn ON display 4 and print
1st digit


__delay_ms(5);s4=0;    //Turn OFF display 4 after
5ms delay
```

This is the genuine spot where the MCU chats with the 7-fragment. As we probably am aware we can show just a single digit at once, yet we have four digits to be shown and just if all the four digits are On the total four digit number will be notable for the client.

Things being what they are, how would we go with this?

Fortunate for us our MCU is especially quicker than a natural eye, so what we really do: we show each digit in turn yet we do it quick as appeared previously.

We select one digit show it hang tight for 5ms so the MCU and 7-portion can process it and afterward turn off that digit and proceed onward to the following digit and do likewise till we arrive at the last digit. This deferral of 5ms can't be seen by a natural eye and all the four digits had all the earmarks of being On simultaneously.

That is it, at long last we just augmentation the estimation of showed digit utilizing a deferral as demonstrated as follows

```
if(flag>=100) //wait till flag reaches 100

{

    i++;flag=0; //only if flag is hundred "i" will be incremented

}

flag++; //increment flag for each flash
```

The postponement is utilized so the time taken for changing starting with one number then onto the next is long enough for us to see the change.

The total code is given underneath toward the end.

Equipment Setup and Testing:

As consistently let us reenact the program utilizing Proteus before we really go with our equipment. In case the reenactment is fruitful you should see like this

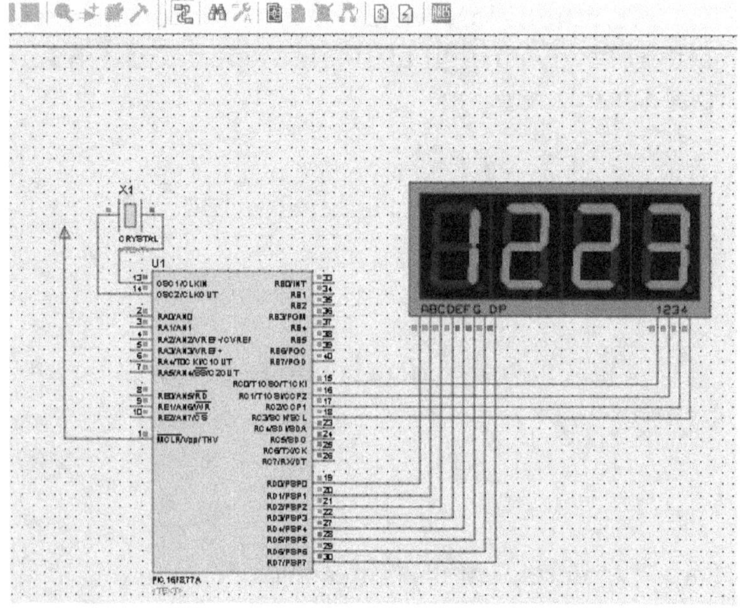

This undertaking doesn't have any confused equipment arrangement, we are again utilizing a similar PIC Microcontroller board which we have made in LED flickering Tutorial. Just associate the 7-portion Module with your PIC Microcontroller board concurring the association chart. When you are finished with the associations, basically dump the code utilizing your PicKit 3 developer and that is it do the most of your yield.

Code

```
// CONFIG
#pragma config FOSC = HS      // Oscillator Selection
bits (HS oscillator)
#pragma config WDTE = OFF      // Watchdog Timer
Enable bit (WDT disabled)
#pragma config PWRTE = ON      // Power-up Timer
Enable bit (PWRT enabled)
#pragma config BOREN = ON      // Brown-out Reset
Enable bit (BOR enabled)
#pragma config LVP = OFF      // Low-Voltage (Sin-
gle-Supply) In-Circuit Serial Programming Enable bit
(RB3 is digital I/O, HV on MCLR must be used for pro-
gramming)
#pragma config CPD = OFF    // Data EEPROM Memory
Code Protection bit (Data EEPROM code protection
off)
#pragma config WRT = OFF      // Flash Program Mem-
ory Write Enable bits (Write protection off; all pro-
gram memory may be written to by EECON control)
#pragma config CP = OFF     // Flash Program Memory
Code Protection bit (Code protection off)

// #pragma config statements should precede project
file includes.
// Use project enums instead of #define for ON and
OFF.

#include <xc.h>
```

```c
//***Define the signal pins of all four displays***//
#define s1 RC0
#define s2 RC1
#define s3 RC2
#define s4 RC3
//***End of definition**////

void main()
{
unsigned int a,b,c,d,e,f,g,h; //just variables
int i = 0; //the 4-digit value that is to be displayed
int flag =0; //for creating delay

unsigned int seg[]={0X3F, //Hex value to display the number 0
        0X06, //Hex value to display the number 1
        0X5B, //Hex value to display the number 2
        0X4F, //Hex value to display the number 3
        0X66, //Hex value to display the number 4
        0X6D, //Hex value to display the number 5
        0X7C, //Hex value to display the number 6
        0X07, //Hex value to display the number 7
        0X7F, //Hex value to display the number 8
        0X6F  //Hex value to display the number 9
        }; //End of Array for displaying numbers from 0 to 9

//*****I/O Configuration****//
TRISC=0X00;
PORTC=0X00;
TRISD=0x00;
PORTD=0X00;
```

```c
//***End of I/O configuration**///

#define _XTAL_FREQ 20000000

while(1)
{
 //***Splitting "i" into four digits***//
a=i%10;//4th digit is saved here
b=i/10;
c=b%10;//3rd digit is saved here
d=b/10;
e=d%10; //2nd digit is saved here
f=d/10;
g=f%10; //1st digit is saved here
h=f/10;
//***End of splitting***//

PORTD=seg[g];s1=1; //Turn ON display 1 and print 4th digit
__delay_ms(5);s1=0;   //Turn OFF display 1 after 5ms delay
PORTD=seg[e];s2=1; //Turn ON display 2 and print 3rd digit
__delay_ms(5);s2=0;   //Turn OFF display 2 after 5ms delay
PORTD=seg[c];s3=1; //Turn ON display 3 and print 2nd digit
__delay_ms(5);s3=0;   //Turn OFF display 3 after 5ms delay
PORTD=seg[a];s4=1; //Turn ON display 4 and print 1st digit
__delay_ms(5);s4=0;   //Turn OFF display 4 after 5ms
```

```
delay

if(flag>=100) //wait till flag reaches 100
{
   i++;flag=0; //only if flag is hundred "i" will be incre-
mented
}
flag++; //increment flag for each flash
}
}
```

◆ ◆ ◆

9. SHOW CUSTOM CHARACTERS ON 16X2 LCD UTILIZING PIC MICROCON-TROLLER AND XC8

In our past instructional exercise, we have figured out How to Interface a 16*2 LCD with PIC Microcontroller. We prescribe you to experience it before going any further, in the event that you are novice in PIC microcontroller. Already we have additionally taken in the rudiments of PIC utilizing LED flickering Program and Timers in PIC Microcontroller. You can check here all the instructional exercises on Learning PIC Microcontrollers utilizing MPLABX along with XC8 compiler.

In this instructional exercise, let us do it all the more fascinating by making our own custom characters along with showing them on our Liquid Crystal Display screen utilizing PIC16F877A PIC Microcontroller. Additionally there are few pre-characterized generally utilized custom characters given by the HD44780A IC itself, we will likewise perceive how we can utilize them. As clarified in our past instructional exercise our LCD has a Hitachi HD44780 controller inserted on it which causes us to show characters. Each character that we show is now pre-characterized inside the ROM of the HD44780 IC. We will find out about Liquid Crystal Display controller IC HD44780, before showing character on Liquid Crystal Display.

16x2 Dot Matrix LCD Controller IC HD44780:

So as to show a custom character, we need to by one way or another tell the IC that how the custom character will resemble. To do that we should think about the Three kinds of Memories present inside the HD44780 LCD controller IC:

Character Generator ROM (CGROM): It is the perused just memory which, as said prior, contains all the examples of the characters pre-characterized inside it. This ROM will fluctuate from each sort of Interface IC, and some may have some pre-characterized custom character with them.

Show Data RAM (DDRAM): This is an irregular access

memory. Each time we show a character its example will be gotten from the CGROM and moved to the DDRAM and afterward will be set on the screen. To put it basic, DDRAM will have the examples of all characters that are right now being shown on the Liquid Crystal Display Screen. Along these lines for each cycle the IC need not get information from CGROM, and aides in getting a short update recurrence

Character generator RAM (CGRAM): This is additionally a Random access memory, so we can compose and peruse information from it. As the name infers this memory will be the one which can used to produce the custom character. We require to shape an example for the character and compose it in the CGRAM, this example can be perused and shown on the Screen when required.

Presently, since we got a fundamental comprehension of the sorts of Memory present in the HD44780 interface IC. Let us investigate its datasheet to comprehend more.

Table 4   Correspondence between Character Codes and Character Patterns (ROM Code: A00)

Lower Bits	Upper Bits	0000	0001	0010	0011	0100	0101	0110	0111	1000	1001	1010	1011	1100	1101	1110	1111
xxxx0000	CG RAM (1)				0	@	P	`	p				ー	タ	ミ	α	p
xxxx0001	(2)			!	1	A	Q	a	q			。	ア	チ	ム	ä	q
xxxx0010	(3)			"	2	B	R	b	r			「	イ	ツ	メ	β	θ
xxxx0011	(4)			#	3	C	S	c	s			」	ウ	テ	モ	ε	∞
xxxx0100	(5)			$	4	D	T	d	t			、	エ	ト	ヤ	μ	Ω
xxxx0101	(6)			%	5	E	U	e	u			・	オ	ナ	ユ	σ	ü
xxxx0110	(7)			&	6	F	V	f	v			ヲ	カ	ニ	ヨ	ρ	Σ
xxxx0111	(8)			'	7	G	W	g	w			ア	キ	ヌ	ラ	g	π
xxxx1000	(1)			(	8	H	X	h	x			ィ	ク	ネ	リ	√	x̄
xxxx1001	(2)			)	9	I	Y	i	y			ゥ	ケ	ノ	ル	⁻¹	y
xxxx1010	(3)			*	:	J	Z	j	z			エ	コ	ハ	レ	j	千
xxxx1011	(4)			+	;	K	[	k	{			オ	サ	ヒ	ロ	×	万
xxxx1100	(5)			,	<	L	¥	l	|			ャ	シ	フ	ワ	¢	円
xxxx1101	(6)			-	=	M	]	m	}			ュ	ス	ヘ	ン	£	÷
xxxx1110	(7)			.	>	N	^	n	→			ョ	セ	ホ	゛	ñ	
xxxx1111	(8)			/	?	O	_	o	←			ッ	ソ	マ	゜	ö	█

Note: The user can specify any pattern for character-generator RAM.

As, the datasheet infers, the HD44780 IC has given as 8 Locations to store our custom examples in CGRAM, additionally on the correct we can see that there are some pre-characterized characters which can likewise be shown on our LCD Screen. Let us perceive how we can do it.

Showing a Custom Character on 16x2 LCD:

To show a custom character we should initially create an example for it and afterward spare it to the

CGRAM. Since we have the library capacities with us as of now, it must be anything but difficult to do this with some basic orders. Here is the Library for LCD capacities, however here we have duplicate glued all the Library capacities in the program itself, so no compelling reason to incorporate this header document in our program. Likewise check this article for Basic LCD working and its Pinouts.

The initial step is to produce an example or the custom character. As we probably am aware each character is a mix of 5*8 specks. We need to choose which spot (pixel) ought to go high and which should remain low. Just draw a container like underneath and conceal the districts dependent on your character. My character here is a stick man (trust it would seem that one). When concealed, straightforward compose the proportionate parallel estimation of every byte as demonstrated as follows.

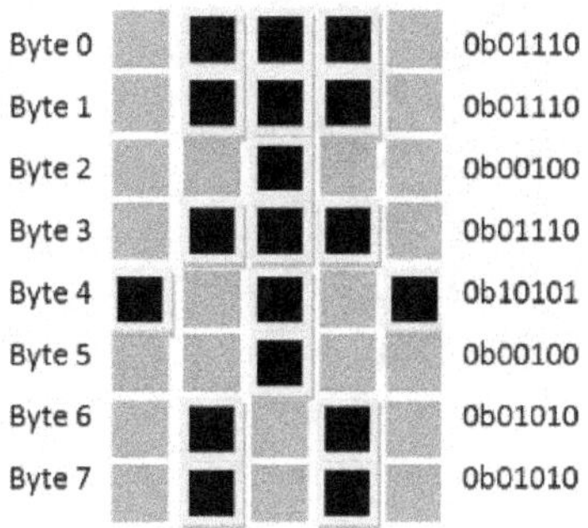

Just put a '1' on the concealed area and a '0' on the unconcealed district for every byte, and that is it our custom example is prepared. Also I have done 8 custom example codes for our 8 memory spaces present it the CGROM. They are recorded in the table underneath.

S.NO:	Custom Character	Pattern Code
1		0b01110, 0b01110, 0b00100, 0b01110, 0b10101, 0b00100, 0b01010, 0b01010
2		0b00000, 0b00000, 0b01010, 0b00100, 0b00100, 0b10001, 0b01110, 0b00000

3		0b00100, 0b01110, 0b11111, 0b11111, 0b01110, 0b01110, 0b01010, 0b01010
4		0b01110, 0b10001, 0b10001, 0b11111, 0b11011, 0b11011, 0b11111, 0b00000
5		0b01110, 0b10000, 0b10000, 0b11111, 0b11011, 0b11011, 0b11111, 0b00000

6		0b00000, 0b10001, 0b01010, 0b10001, 0b00100, 0b01110, 0b10001, 0b00000
7		0b00000, 0b00000, 0b01010, 0b10101, 0b10001, 0b01110, 0b00100, 0b00000
8		0b11111, 0b11111, 0b10101, 0b11011, 0b11011, 0b11111, 0b10001, 0b11111

Note: It isn't required to stack all the 8 spaces gave in the CGRAM.

Programming and Working Explanation:

Presently our example codes are prepared, we simply need to stack them to the CGRAM of LCD and show them utilizing PIC microcontroller. To stack them in to the CGRAM we can frame a 5*8 exhibit of components and burden every byte by utilizing a 'for circle'. The variety of example code is demonstrated as follows:

```
const unsigned short Custom_Char5x8[] = {

 0b01110,0b01110,0b00100,0b01110,0b10101,
0b00100,0b01010,0b01010, // Code for CGRAM
memory space 1

 0b00000,0b00000,0b01010,0b00100,0b00100,
0b10001,0b01110,0b00000, // Code for CGRAM
memory space 2

 0b00100,0b01110,0b11111,0b11111,0b01110,
0b01110,0b01010,0b01010, // Code for CGRAM
memory space 3

 0b01110,0b10001,0b10001,0b11111,0b11011,
0b11011,0b11111,0b00000, // Code for CGRAM
memory space 4
```

```
  0b01110,0b10000,0b10000,0b11111,0b11011,
0b11011,0b11111,0b00000, // Code for CGRAM
memory space 5

  0b00000,0b10001,0b01010,0b10001,0b00100,
0b01110,0b10001,0b00000, // Code for CGRAM
memory space 6

  0b00000,0b00000,0b01010,0b10101,0b10001,
0b01110,0b00100,0b00000, // Code for CGRAM
memory space 7

  0b11111,0b11111,0b10101,0b11011,0b11011,
0b11111,0b10001,0b11111  // Code for CGRAM
memory space 8

};
```

Every memory space is stacked with its regarded character design. To stack this example into the HD44780 IC, the information sheet of HD44780 must be alluded, yet it is simply lines of order that can be utilized to set the location of the CGRAM

```
//*** Load custom char into the CGROM***//////

  Lcd_Cmd(0x04);  // Set CGRAM Address

  Lcd_Cmd(0x00);  // .. set CGRAM Address
```

```
for (i = 0; i <= 63 ; i++)

  Lcd_Print_Char(Custom_Char5x8[i]);

Lcd_Cmd(0);    // Return to Home

Lcd_Cmd(2);    // .. return to Home

//*** Loading custom char complete***//////
```

Here, inside the 'for circle' every twofold worth is stacked into the CGROM. When the example is stacked, the custom characters can be made to show by essentially calling the area of the example utilizing the void Lcd_Print_Char(char information) work as demonstrated as follows.

```
Lcd_Print_Char(0); // Display Custom Character 0

Lcd_Print_Char(1); // Display Custom Character
1

Lcd_Print_Char(2); // Display Custom Character
2

Lcd_Print_Char(3); // Display Custom Character
3

Lcd_Print_Char(4); // Display Custom Character
```

```
4

    Lcd_Print_Char(5); // Display Custom Character
5

    Lcd_Print_Char(6); // Display Custom Character
6

    Lcd_Print_Char(7); // Display Custom Character
7
```

Print Predefined Special Character:

The HD44780 IC has some predefined extraordinary characters put away in the DDROM. These characters can be straightforwardly imprinted on to the screen by alluding to its paired an incentive in the datasheet.

For instance: The parallel estimation of the character "ALPHA" is 0b11100000. Step at a time instructions to acquire this can be comprehended from the figure beneath, in like manner you can get an incentive for any unique character which is pre-characterized in the IC.

Table 4   Correspondence between Character Codes and Character Patterns (ROM Code: A00)

Lower 4 bits (Upper 4 bits →)		0000	0001	0010	0011	0100	0101	0110	0111	1000	1001	1010	1011	1100	1101	1110	1111
xxxx0000	(1)	CG RAM (1)			0	@	P	`	p				ー	タ	ミ	α	p
xxxx0001	(2)			!	1	A	Q	a	q			。	ア	チ	ム	ä	q
xxxx0010	(3)			"	2	B	R	b	r			「	イ	ツ	メ	β	θ
xxxx0011	(4)			#	3	C	S	c	s			」	ウ	テ	モ	ε	∞
xxxx0100	(5)			$	4	D	T	d	t			、	エ	ト	ヤ	μ	Ω
xxxx0101	(6)			%	5	E	U	e	u			・	オ	ナ	ユ	σ	ü
xxxx0110	(7)			&	6	F	V	f	v			ヲ	カ	ニ	ヨ	ρ	Σ
xxxx0111	(8)			'	7	G	W	g	w			ア	キ	ヌ	ラ	g	π
xxxx1000	(1)			(	8	H	X	h	x			ィ	ク	ネ	リ	√	x̄
xxxx1001	(2)			)	9	I	Y	i	y			ゥ	ケ	ノ	ル	⁻¹	y
xxxx1010	(3)			*	:	J	Z	j	z			エ	コ	ハ	レ	j	千
xxxx1011	(4)			+	;	K	[	k	{			オ	サ	ヒ	ロ	×	万
xxxx1100	(5)			,	<	L	¥	l	|			ャ	シ	フ	ワ	¢	円
xxxx1101	(6)			-	=	M	]	m	}			ュ	ス	ヘ	ン	£	÷
xxxx1110	(7)			.	>	N	^	n	→			ョ	セ	ホ	゛	ñ	
xxxx1111	(8)			/	?	O	_	o	←			ッ	ソ	マ	゜	ö	█

Note: The user can specify any pattern for character-generator RAM.

When the paired worth is known, the relating character can be printed to the screen by essentially utilizing the void Lcd_Print_Char(char information) work as demonstrated as follows,

```
Lcd_Print_Char(0b11100000); //binary value of alpha from data-sheet
```

Circuit Connections and Testing:

This undertaking doesn't have any extra equipment

necessity, we have just utilized similar associations from the past LCD interfacing instructional exercise and utilized a similar board which we have made in LED squinting Tutorial. As forever we should reproduce the program utilizing Proteus to confirm our yield.

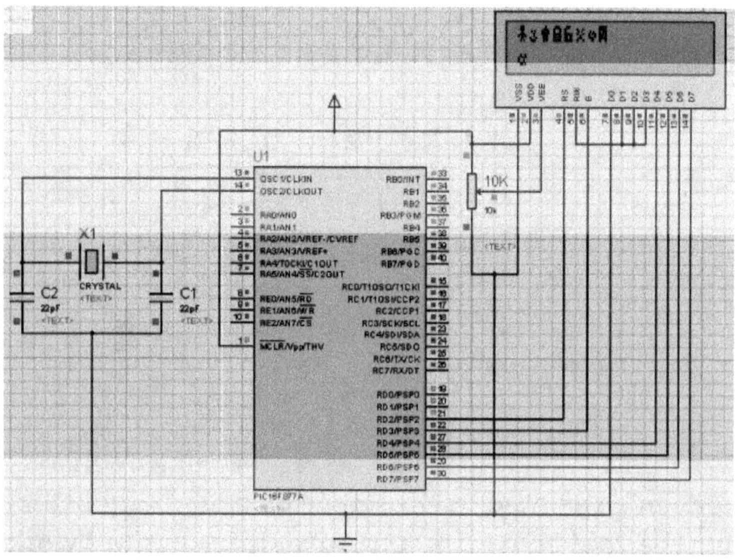

When we have are reenactment running true to form, lets straightforwardly consume the code into our Hardware set-up. The yield of the program ought to be something like this:

So's the manner by which you can Display any Custom Character on 16x2 LCD utilizing PIC Microcontroller with MPLABX along with XC8 compiler. Likewise check our total PIC Microcontroller Learning Series here.

Code

```
#define _XTAL_FREQ 20000000

#define RS RD2
#define EN RD3
#define D4 RD4
```

```c
#define D5 RD5
#define D6 RD6
#define D7 RD7

#include <xc.h>

#pragma config FOSC = HS      // Oscillator Selection
bits (HS oscillator)
#pragma config WDTE = OFF       // Watchdog Timer
Enable bit (WDT disabled)
#pragma config PWRTE = ON       // Power-up Timer
Enable bit (PWRT enabled)
#pragma config BOREN = ON       // Brown-out Reset
Enable bit (BOR enabled)
#pragma config LVP = OFF        // Low-Voltage (Sin-
gle-Supply) In-Circuit Serial Programming Enable bit
(RB3 is digital I/O, HV on MCLR must be used for pro-
gramming)
#pragma config CPD = OFF    // Data EEPROM Memory
Code Protection bit (Data EEPROM code protection
off)
#pragma config WRT = OFF     // Flash Program Mem-
ory Write Enable bits (Write protection off; all pro-
gram memory may be written to by EECON control)
#pragma config CP = OFF     // Flash Program Memory
Code Protection bit (Code protection off)

//LCD Functions

/*******START OF LCD FUNCTIONS*********/
void Lcd_SetBit(char data_bit) //Based on the Hex
value Set the Bits of the Data Lines
{
```

```
  if(data_bit& 1)
    D4 = 1;
  else
    D4 = 0;

  if(data_bit& 2)
    D5 = 1;
  else
    D5 = 0;

  if(data_bit& 4)
    D6 = 1;
  else
    D6 = 0;

  if(data_bit& 8)
    D7 = 1;
  else
    D7 = 0;
}

void Lcd_Cmd(char a)
{
  RS = 0;
  Lcd_SetBit(a); //Incoming Hex value
  EN = 1;
    __delay_ms(4);
    EN = 0;
}

Lcd_Clear()
{
  Lcd_Cmd(0); //Clear the LCD
```

```c
  Lcd_Cmd(1); //Move the curser to first position
}

void Lcd_Set_Cursor(char a, char b)
{
  char temp,z,y;
  if(a== 1)
  {
     temp = 0x80 + b - 1; //80H is used to move the curser
    z = temp>>4; //Lower 8-bits
    y = temp & 0x0F; //Upper 8-bits
    Lcd_Cmd(z); //Set Row
    Lcd_Cmd(y); //Set Column
  }
  else if(a== 2)
  {
    temp = 0xC0 + b - 1;
    z = temp>>4; //Lower 8-bits
    y = temp & 0x0F; //Upper 8-bits
    Lcd_Cmd(z); //Set Row
    Lcd_Cmd(y); //Set Column
  }
}

void Lcd_Start()
{
 Lcd_SetBit(0x00);
 for(int i=1065244; i<=0; i--) NOP();
 Lcd_Cmd(0x03);
  __delay_ms(5);
 Lcd_Cmd(0x03);
```

```
  __delay_ms(11);
 Lcd_Cmd(0x03);
  Lcd_Cmd(0x02); //02H is used for Return home ->
Clears the RAM and initializes the LCD
  Lcd_Cmd(0x02); //02H is used for Return home ->
Clears the RAM and initializes the LCD
 Lcd_Cmd(0x08); //Select Row 1
 Lcd_Cmd(0x00); //Clear Row 1 Display
 Lcd_Cmd(0x0C); //Select Row 2
 Lcd_Cmd(0x00); //Clear Row 2 Display
 Lcd_Cmd(0x06);
}

void  Lcd_Print_Char(char  data)     //Send  8-bits
through 4-bit mode
{
 char Lower_Nibble,Upper_Nibble;
 Lower_Nibble = data&0x0F;
 Upper_Nibble = data&0xF0;
 RS = 1;       // => RS = 1
  Lcd_SetBit(Upper_Nibble>>4);        //Send upper
half by shifting by 4
 EN = 1;
 for(int i=2130483; i<=0; i--) NOP();
 EN = 0;
 Lcd_SetBit(Lower_Nibble); //Send Lower half
 EN = 1;
 for(int i=2130483; i<=0; i--) NOP();
 EN = 0;
}

void Lcd_Print_String(char *a)
```

```c
{
  int i;
  for(i=0;a[i]!='\0';i++)
      Lcd_Print_Char(a[i]);   //Split the string using
pointers and call the Char function
}
```

/*******END OF LCD FUNCTIONS*********/
const unsigned short Custom_Char5x8[] = {

0b01110,0b01110,0b00100,0b01110,0b10101,0b00100,0b01010,0b01010, // Code for CGRAM memory space 1

0b00000,0b00000,0b01010,0b00100,0b00100,0b10001,0b01110,0b00000, // Code for CGRAM memory space 2

0b00100,0b01110,0b11111,0b11111,0b01110,0b01110,0b01010,0b01010, // Code for CGRAM memory space 3

0b01110,0b10001,0b10001,0b11111,0b11011,0b11011,0b11111,0b00000, // Code for CGRAM memory space 4

0b01110,0b10000,0b10000,0b11111,0b11011,0b11011,0b11111,0b00000, // Code for CGRAM memory space 5

0b00000,0b10001,0b01010,0b10001,0b00100,0b0

```c
1110,0b10001,0b00000, // Code for CGRAM memory
space 6

0b00000,0b00000,0b01010,0b10101,0b10001,0b0
1110,0b00100,0b00000, // Code for CGRAM memory
space 7

0b11111,0b11111,0b10101,0b11011,0b11011,0b1
1111,0b10001,0b11111 // Code for CGRAM memory
space 8
};

int main()
{
  unsigned int a;char i;
  TRISD = 0x00;
  Lcd_Start();


   //*** Load custom char into the CGROM***//////
  Lcd_Cmd(0x04);  // Set CGRAM Address
  Lcd_Cmd(0x00);  //.. set CGRAM Address
  for (i = 0; i <= 63 ; i++)
   Lcd_Print_Char(Custom_Char5x8[i]);
  Lcd_Cmd(0);   // Return to Home
  Lcd_Cmd(2);   //.. return to Home
  //*** Loading custom char complete***//////


   while(1)
  {
    Lcd_Clear();
```

```c
   //Print all Custom characters//
 Lcd_Set_Cursor(1,1);
 Lcd_Print_Char(0); // Display Custom Character 0
 Lcd_Print_Char(1); // Display Custom Character 1
 Lcd_Print_Char(2); // Display Custom Character 2
 Lcd_Print_Char(3); // Display Custom Character 3
 Lcd_Print_Char(4); // Display Custom Character 4
 Lcd_Print_Char(5); // Display Custom Character 5
 Lcd_Print_Char(6); // Display Custom Character 6
 Lcd_Print_Char(7); // Display Custom Character 7


   //Print predefined special character//
 Lcd_Set_Cursor(2,1);
   Lcd_Print_Char(0b11100000); //binary value of
alpha from data-sheet
 __delay_ms(1000);
 }
 return 0;
}
```

❖ ❖ ❖

10. LCD INTERFACING WITH PIC MICROCONTROLLER UTILIZING MPLABX AND XC8

This is our 6th instructional exercise in our PIC Tutorial Series, in this instructional exercise we get the hang of Interfacing of 16x2 LCD with PIC Microcontroller. In our past instructional exercises we have taken in the fundamentals of PIC utilizing some LED squinting Programs and have additionally figured out How to utilize Timers in PIC Microcontroller. You can check here all the instructional exercises on Learning PIC Microcontrollers utilizing MPLABX and XC8 compiler.

This instructional exercise will be a fascinating one

since we will figure out How to Interface 16×2 LCD with PIC16F877A. Gone are the past times where we utilized LEDs for client signs. Let us perceive how we can do our activities look progressively cool and helpful by utilizing LCD shows. Additionally check our past articles on Interfacing LCD with 8051, with Arduino, with Raspberry Pi, with AVR.

Capacities for Interfacing Liquid Crystal Display with PIC Microcontroller:

To make things simpler we have made a little library that could make things simple while utilizing this Liquid Crystal Display with our PIC16F877A. The header document "MyLCD.h" is given here for download, which contains all the fundamental capacity to drive the LCD utilizing PIC MCU. Library code is all around clarified by remark lines however on the off chance that you despite everything have questions contact us through the remark area. Additionally check this article for Basic Liquid Crystal Display working along with its Pinouts.

Note: It is constantly prescribed to recognize what is really occurring inside your header record since it will help you in investigating or while changing the MCU.

Presently, there are 2 different ways to include this code into your program. You can either duplicate all the above lines of code in MyLCD.h and glue them before the void primary(). Or simultaneously you can download the header document utilizing the connection and add them to the header record of your task (#include " MyLCD.h ";). This should be possible by right tapping on the header record and choosing Add existing Item and perusing to this header document.

Here I have reordered the header document code into my principle C record. So in case you are using our code, in this point you don't have to download and include the header record into your program, simply utilize the total Code given toward the finish of this Tutorial. Likewise note that this library will just help PIC16F arrangement PIC Microcontroller.

Here I am clarifying each capacity inside our header record beneath:

void Lcd_Start(): This capacity ought to be the primary capacity that must be called to begin working with our LCD. We should call this capacity just a single time to dodge slack in the program.

```
void Lcd_Start()

{

Lcd_SetBit(0x00);

for(int i=1065244; i<=0; i--) NOP();
```

```
  Lcd_Cmd(0x03);

   __delay_ms(5);

  Lcd_Cmd(0x03);

   __delay_ms(11);

  Lcd_Cmd(0x03);

  Lcd_Cmd(0x02); //02H is used for Return home ->
Clears the RAM and initializes the LCD

  Lcd_Cmd(0x02); //02H is used for Return home ->
Clears the RAM and initializes the LCD

  Lcd_Cmd(0x08); //Select Row 1

  Lcd_Cmd(0x00); //Clear Row 1 Display

  Lcd_Cmd(0x0C); //Select Row 2

  Lcd_Cmd(0x00); //Clear Row 2 Display

  Lcd_Cmd(0x06);

}
```

Lcd_Clear(): This capacity clears the LCD screen and can be utilized inside circles to free the appearance from past information.

```
Lcd_Clear()

{

    Lcd_Cmd(0); //Clear the LCD

    Lcd_Cmd(1); //Move the cursor to first position

}
```

void Lcd_Set_Cursor(x pos, y pos): Once began, our LCD is prepared to take orders, we can teach the LCD to set its cursor in you favored area by utilizing this capacity. Assume in the event that, we need out cursor at fifth character of first column. At that point the capacity will be void Lcd_Set_Cursor(1, 5)

```
void Lcd_Set_Cursor(char a, char b)

{

    char temp,z,y;

    if(a== 1)

    {
```

```c
    temp = 0x80 + b - 1; //80H is used to move the cursor

    z = temp>>4; //Lower 8-bits

    y = temp & 0x0F; //Upper 8-bits

    Lcd_Cmd(z); //Set Row

    Lcd_Cmd(y); //Set Column

}

else if(a== 2)

{

    temp = 0xC0 + b - 1;

    z = temp>>4; //Lower 8-bits

    y = temp & 0x0F; //Upper 8-bits

    Lcd_Cmd(z); //Set Row

    Lcd_Cmd(y); //Set Column

}
}
```

void Lcd_Print_Char(char information) : Once the cursor is set we can compose a character to its situation by basic calling this capacity.

```
void  Lcd_Print_Char(char  data)    //Send  8-bits
through 4-bit mode

{

  char Lower_Nibble,Upper_Nibble;

  Lower_Nibble = data&0x0F;

  Upper_Nibble = data&0xF0;

  RS = 1;       // => RS = 1

  Lcd_SetBit(Upper_Nibble>>4);       //Send upper
half by shifting by 4

  EN = 1;

  for(int i=2130483;i<=0;i--) NOP();

  EN = 0;

  Lcd_SetBit(Lower_Nibble); //Send Lower half

  EN = 1;
```

```
  for(int i=2130483;i<=0;i--) NOP();

  EN = 0;


}
```

void Lcd_Print_String(char *a): If a gathering of characters is to be shown, at that point the string capacity can be utilized.

```
void Lcd_Print_String(char *a)

{

  int i;

  for(i=0;a[i]!='\0';i++)

    Lcd_Print_Char(a[i]);   //Split the string using
  pointers and call the Char function


}
```

Each time the Lcd_Print_Char(char information) is called, its particular character esteems is sent to the information lines of the Liquid Crystal Display. These characters arrive at the HD44780U in type of bits. Presently this IC relates the bits to the character to be shown by utilizing its ROM memory as indicated the underneath table. You can discover bits for all the characters in the datasheet of HD44780U Liquid Crystal Display Controller.

Lower 4 Bits \ Upper 4 Bits	0000	0001	0010	0011	0100	0101	0110	0111	1000	1001	1010	1011	1100	1101	1110	1111
xxxx0000	CG RAM (1)			0	@	P	`	p				—	タ	ミ	α	p
xxxx0001	(2)		!	1	A	Q	a	q			。	ア	チ	ム	ä	q
xxxx0010	(3)		"	2	B	R	b	r			「	イ	ツ	メ	β	θ
xxxx0011	(4)		#	3	C	S	c	s			」	ウ	テ	モ	ε	∞
xxxx0100	(5)		$	4	D	T	d	t			、	エ	ト	ヤ	μ	Ω
xxxx0101	(6)		%	5	E	U	e	u			・	オ	ナ	ユ	σ	ü
xxxx0110	(7)		&	6	F	V	f	v			ヲ	カ	ニ	ヨ	ρ	Σ
xxxx0111	(8)		'	7	G	W	g	w			ア	キ	ヌ	ラ	g	π
xxxx1000	(1)		(	8	H	X	h	x			ィ	ク	ネ	リ	√	x̄
xxxx1001	(2)		)	9	I	Y	i	y			ゥ	ケ	ノ	ル	⁻¹	y
xxxx1010	(3)		*	:	J	Z	j	z			ェ	コ	ハ	レ	j	千
xxxx1011	(4)		+	;	K	[	k	{			ォ	サ	ヒ	ロ	ˣ	万
xxxx1100	(5)		,	<	L	¥	l	|			ャ	シ	フ	ワ	¢	円
xxxx1101	(6)		-	=	M	]	m	}			ュ	ス	ヘ	ン	£	÷
xxxx1110	(7)		.	>	N	^	n	→			ョ	セ	ホ	゛	ñ	
xxxx1111	(8)		/	?	O	_	o	←			ッ	ソ	マ	゜	ö	█

Note: The user can specify any pattern for character-generator RAM.

Presently, since we are happy with our header record we should fabricate the circuit and test the program. Additionally check total header document given in the connection given previously.

Circuit Diagram and Testing:

The following is the circuit outline for Interfacing 16x2 Liquid Crystal Display with PIC Microcontroller.

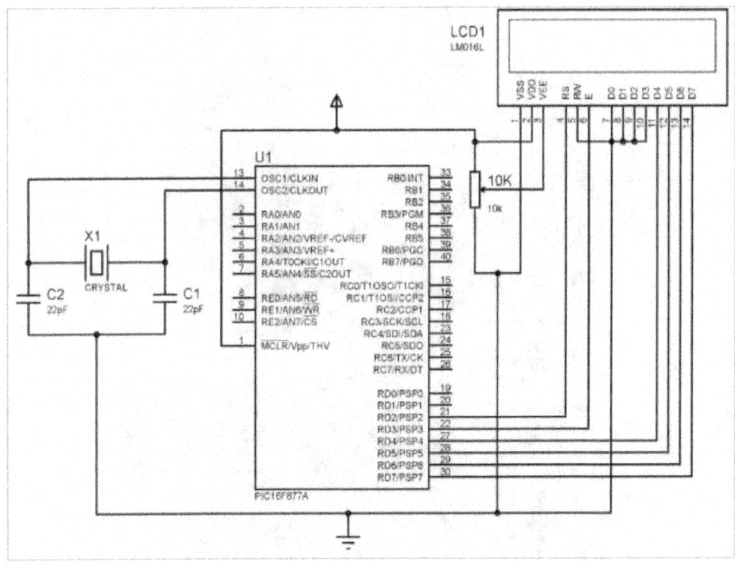

I have not indicated the Power flexibly or ICSP association in the above circuit, since we are utilizing a similar board which we have utilized in past instructional exercise, check here.

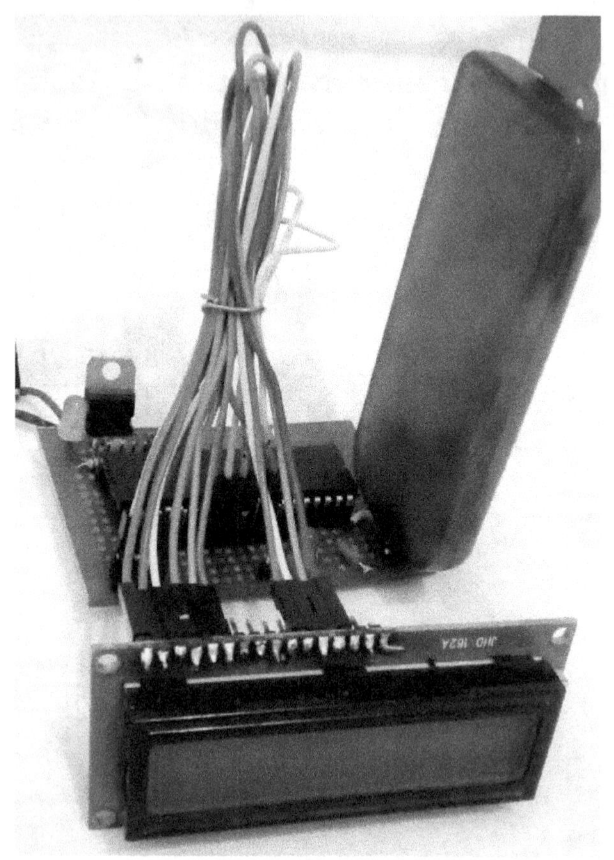

One significant thing to see in the program is the pin meanings of LCD:

```
#define RS RD2

#define EN RD3

#define D4 RD4
```

```
#define D5 RD5

#define D6 RD6

#define D7 RD7
```

These pin definitions can be changed by the software engineers equipment arrangement. Make sure to change the regarded port setup in the fundamental capacity on the off chance that you change here.

The equipment for this task is exceptionally straightforward. We will reuse a similar PIC module that we utilized last time and associate the LCD module to our PIC utilizing jumper wires.

The association can be comprehended by the accompanying table:

LCD Pin No.	LCD Pin Name	MCU Pin Name	MCU Pin No.
1	Ground	Ground	12
2	VCC	+5V	11
3	VEE	Ground	12
4	Register Select	RD2	21

5	Read/Write	Ground	12
6	Enable	RD3	22
7	Data Bit 0	NC	-
8	Data Bit 1	NC	-
9	Data Bit 2	NC	-
10	Data Bit 3	NC	-
11	Data Bit 4	RD4	27
12	Data Bit 5	RD5	28
13	Data Bit 6	RD6	29
14	Data Bit 7	RD7	30
15	LED Positive	+5V	11
16	LED Negative	Ground	12

Presently let us essentially make the associations, dump the code to our MCU and confirm the yield.

Code

```
#define _XTAL_FREQ 20000000

#define RS RD2
#define EN RD3
#define D4 RD4
#define D5 RD5
#define D6 RD6
#define D7 RD7

#include <xc.h>
```

```
#pragma config FOSC = HS      // Oscillator Selection
bits (HS oscillator)
#pragma config WDTE = OFF      // Watchdog Timer
Enable bit (WDT disabled)
#pragma config PWRTE = ON      // Power-up Timer
Enable bit (PWRT enabled)
#pragma config BOREN = ON      // Brown-out Reset
Enable bit (BOR enabled)
#pragma config LVP = OFF       // Low-Voltage (Sin-
gle-Supply) In-Circuit Serial Programming Enable bit
(RB3 is digital I/O, HV on MCLR must be used for pro-
gramming)
#pragma config CPD = OFF    // Data EEPROM Memory
Code Protection bit (Data EEPROM code protection
off)
#pragma config WRT = OFF     // Flash Program Mem-
ory Write Enable bits (Write protection off; all pro-
gram memory may be written to by EECON control)
#pragma config CP = OFF      // Flash Program Memory
Code Protection bit (Code protection off)

//LCD Functions
void Lcd_SetBit(char data_bit) //Based on the Hex
value Set the Bits of the Data Lines
{
  if(data_bit& 1)
    D4 = 1;
  else
    D4 = 0;

  if(data_bit& 2)
    D5 = 1;
```

```
    else
      D5 = 0;

  if(data_bit& 4)
      D6 = 1;
  else
      D6 = 0;

  if(data_bit& 8)
      D7 = 1;
  else
      D7 = 0;
}

void Lcd_Cmd(char a)
{
  RS = 0;
  Lcd_SetBit(a); //Incoming Hex value
  EN = 1;
    __delay_ms(4);
    EN = 0;
}

Lcd_Clear()
{
  Lcd_Cmd(0); //Clear the LCD
  Lcd_Cmd(1); //Move the curser to first position
}

void Lcd_Set_Cursor(char a, char b)
{
  char temp,z,y;
  if(a== 1)
```

```c
{
    temp = 0x80 + b - 1; //80H is used to move the curser
    z = temp>>4; //Lower 8-bits
    y = temp & 0x0F; //Upper 8-bits
    Lcd_Cmd(z); //Set Row
    Lcd_Cmd(y); //Set Column
  }
  else if(a==2)
  {
    temp = 0xC0 + b - 1;
    z = temp>>4; //Lower 8-bits
    y = temp & 0x0F; //Upper 8-bits
    Lcd_Cmd(z); //Set Row
    Lcd_Cmd(y); //Set Column
  }
}

void Lcd_Start()
{
 Lcd_SetBit(0x00);
 for(int i=1065244; i<=0; i--) NOP();
 Lcd_Cmd(0x03);
  __delay_ms(5);
 Lcd_Cmd(0x03);
  __delay_ms(11);
 Lcd_Cmd(0x03);
 Lcd_Cmd(0x02); //02H is used for Return home -> Clears the RAM and initializes the LCD
  Lcd_Cmd(0x02); //02H is used for Return home -> Clears the RAM and initializes the LCD
```

```c
Lcd_Cmd(0x08); //Select Row 1
Lcd_Cmd(0x00); //Clear Row 1 Display
Lcd_Cmd(0x0C); //Select Row 2
Lcd_Cmd(0x00); //Clear Row 2 Display
Lcd_Cmd(0x06);
}

void Lcd_Print_Char(char data)     //Send 8-bits through 4-bit mode
{
  char Lower_Nibble,Upper_Nibble;
  Lower_Nibble = data&0x0F;
  Upper_Nibble = data&0xF0;
  RS = 1;        // => RS = 1
  Lcd_SetBit(Upper_Nibble>>4);         //Send upper half by shifting by 4
  EN = 1;
  for(int i=2130483;i<=0;i--) NOP();
  EN = 0;
  Lcd_SetBit(Lower_Nibble); //Send Lower half
  EN = 1;
  for(int i=2130483;i<=0;i--) NOP();
  EN = 0;
}

void Lcd_Print_String(char *a)
{
  int i;
  for(i=0;a[i]!='\0';i++)
      Lcd_Print_Char(a[i]);  //Split the string using pointers and call the Char function
}
```

```c
int main()
{
  unsigned int a;
  TRISD = 0x00;
  Lcd_Start();
  while(1)
  {
   Lcd_Clear();
   Lcd_Set_Cursor(1,1);
   Lcd_Print_String("Hello world");
   Lcd_Set_Cursor(2,1);
   Lcd_Print_String("WORKING!!");
   __delay_ms(2000);
  }
  return 0;
}
```

THANK YOU

www.ingramcontent.com/pod-product-compliance
Lightning Source LLC
Chambersburg PA
CBHW071403150726
48000CB00001B/148